10-MINUTE IDEAS
FOR EARLY YEARS

Cookery fun

Sally Gray

■ **Quick activities for any time of the day**
■ **Links to Early Learning Goals** ■ **Time-saving photocopiables**

Credits

Author
Sally Gray

Editor
Roanne Charles

Assistant Editor
Andrea Lewis

Series Designer
Anna Oliwa

Designer
Andrea Lewis

Cover Illustration
Craig Cameron/Art Collection

Illustrations
Debbie Clark

Text © Sally Gray 2005
© 2005 Scholastic Ltd

Designed using Adobe InDesign

Published by Scholastic Ltd
Villiers House
Clarendon Avenue
Leamington Spa
Warwickshire
CV32 5PR

www.scholastic.co.uk

Printed by Bell & Bain

1 2 3 4 5 6 7 8 9   5 6 7 8 9 0 1 2 3 4

British Library Cataloguing-in-Publication Data
A catalogue record for this book is available from the British Library.

ISBN 0-439-97171-3
ISBN 978-0439-97171-3

Acknowledgments

The publishers gratefully acknowledge Sally Scott for the use of 'Five a day' © 2005, Sally Scott, previously unpublished and Brenda Williams for the use of 'Apples are…' © 2005, Brenda Williams, previously unpublished (2005, Scholastic Ltd).

Contents

Contents

Festivals and celebrations

Sweet treats

Photocopiables

Introduction

Cooking is fun! And no more so than in the eyes of a young child! Young children love to take part in tactile activities; they love to make things, they love to explore colour, shape and texture, and they love to eat tasty food! Cookery has always been a part of the early years setting, and although it has had periods where it was out of fashion (there was a time when it was perceived to have little educational value), it has remained one of the most motivating learning tools an early years educator can possess!

Making the most of your cookery activities

So where is the learning potential in cookery activities? We all know that children can get some mathematical benefit from learning how to weigh or count out ingredients – but what about the other five areas of the early years curriculum? The activities in this book will show you how to cover all the areas of learning while following some delicious and easy to manage recipes. And all in ten minutes (not including the time taken to cook, of course!).

Planning the environment

The secret of a smooth running, stress-free cookery activity is in the planning – and an organised environment is the key to this. You cannot afford to leave children near a hot oven, or with a sharp knife nearby while you go to get an ingredient that you have forgotten. Each activity in this book begins with a list of 'What you need'. This is broken down into two sections – ingredients and equipment. Make sure that you have easy access to all these things before you begin the activity with the children.

Hygiene and safety

Hygiene and safety are two very important aspects of planning your cookery environment and activities. Make sure that the equipment and the surfaces are spotlessly clean. Don't forget to ask the children to wash their hands and talk to them about basic hygiene rules, such as not licking spoons (or worse, knives) during the cookery activity. From a safety perspective, the two main dangers are sharp knives and implements, and hot ovens/hobs. Make sure that the children are closely supervised when near this equipment. You will also need to talk to them about the dangers of electrical equipment, such as whisks and blenders.

> Be aware of any food allergies and dietary requirements before starting the activities.

How to use this book

This book has been divided into six themed chapters, with each chapter covering all six of the Areas of Learning for the Foundation Stage. The book contains a broad and even spread of the curriculum areas (with weighting towards the areas of Personal, social and emotional development, Communication, language and literacy and Mathematical development in line with the QCA guidelines). The intended outcomes of each activity identify both the Early Learning Goal and a relevant Stepping Stone that can support it, as found in the QCA Curriculum Guidance for the Foundation Stage.

It is not necessary to run the activities in any particular order, and just like any cookery book, you may pick out certain recipes at random to suit current topics, tastes or skills that you wish to target. Chapter 4, Nutritious snacks will provide you with ten suggestions for ways to enhance your snack time and can form part of a topic on Healthy living. Naturally the recipes in Chapter 5, Festivals and celebrations will be best used at the relevant times throughout the year.

All the recipes in the book have been chosen carefully, so as not to be too ambitious or difficult to resource. Each recipe has something for all ages and abilities as well as a section entitled 'Support and extension' which will give you suggestions for ways to help younger or less able children as well as ways to challenge the children further.

Planning for the Stepping Stones and Early Learning Goals

When you delve deeper into the process of following a recipe and creating tasty dishes it is easy to see how learning from cookery can cover all aspects of the Early Years curriculum. Working as part of a group and trying new experiences are just some of the Personal, social and emotional development experiences they will have; in Mathematical development the children will, for example, be weighing and counting out ingredients and making and recognising shapes (see Mini salmon quiches, page 42). Writing out recipes, making a food alphabet (see Chicken burritos, page 40), and making rhyming strings (see French onion dip, page 30) are some of the ways that their language skills will be developed. Learning about festivals and foods from around the world (Chapter 5); rolling out dough (see Pizza dough, page 34) and role-playing a traditional tea party based around a story (see Traditional teabread, page 35) are just some further ways that the remaining curriculum areas can be covered.

Photocopiable pages

There are 14 photocopiable activity pages at the end of the book, linked to the activities. The pages provide a time-saving selection of activities for the children to do; songs and rhymes, re-usable templates and recipes to follow.

Home links

Each activity in this book has a suggestion for ways to link to the children's home environment. This learning partnership provides the ideal environment for the children to learn in – parents and carers can share in the children's progress, and learning will be reinforced at home.

Assessment

Some of the photocopiable pages may be kept for the benefit of assessment and record keeping, helping to provide evidence of a child's level of understanding. These pages are particularly valuable if they are annotated with an adult's observations of the child's approach to learning, as well as with any quotes that highlight their achievements and understanding.

Fruit and vegetables

The recipes and activities in this chapter use fruit and vegetables in imaginative ways to promote a healthy and nutritious diet. While the children are cooking and preparing the food they will be developing a range of other skills, from counting and recognising shapes to using tools and responding to instructions.

Lettuce parcels

What you need
Ingredients: large lettuce leaves, washed; ingredients for the fillings listed on photocopiable sheet 'Parcel fillings' on page 67.
Equipment: mixing bowls; spoons; knives; forks; plates; cooker.

What to do
Ask the children to tell you about their favourite sandwich fillings. Explain that they will be making a special kind of sandwich called a lettuce parcel, using lettuce to wrap the filling instead of bread. Read out the recipes from the photocopiable page and ask the children to decide which filling they would like to put inside their lettuce leaf.

Ask the children to wash their hands, then help them to mix and prepare their chosen filling. Talk about anything that needs to be cooked first and encourage the children to select the ingredients and equipment independently. Provide help as the children select the quantities, and guidance on how to combine, mix or chop the ingredients.

When the children have prepared their sandwich fillings show them how to put a spoonful inside a large washed lettuce leaf and roll it up into a sausage shape. Place on a plate and enjoy!

Support and extension
Chop any ingredients for younger children, but encourage them to do the mixing and spooning out. Suggest that older children invent a different filling, and decide on the ingredients and equipment they will need.

Further ideas
■ Make other roll-up sandwiches using tortilla breads.
■ Cut the lettuce parcels into three or four segments and encourage the children to try each other's creations!
■ Find out about other recipes that involve wrapping foods, such as stuffed vine leaves (a traditional Greek dish), Yuk Sung, and Yeubing or 'Moon cakes' (a traditional Chinese dish, see page 47).

LEARNING OBJECTIVES
STEPPING STONE
Take initiatives and manage developmentally appropriate tasks.

EARLY LEARNING GOAL
Select and use activities and resources independently. (PSED)

GROUP SIZE
Up to five children at a time.

HOME LINKS
Keep in touch with parents and carers about new foods that the children try in your care. Make sure that you have a list of foods that the children are not allowed due to allergies, or for dietary or cultural reasons.

Tasty spuds

LEARNING OBJECTIVES
STEPPING STONE
Have a positive approach to new experiences.

EARLY LEARNING GOAL
Be confident to try new activities, initiate ideas and speak in a familiar group. (PSED)

GROUP SIZE
Up to five children at a time.

What you need
Ingredients: new potatoes; cooking oil; ingredients for the fillings listed on photocopiable sheet 'Parcel fillings' on page 67.
Equipment: baking tin; forks; knives; mixing bowls; serving dishes; spoons; large plates; vegetable brush; kitchen roll; oven.

What to do
Find out if any of the children have eaten baked or 'jacket' potatoes before. If so, what are their favourite fillings? Do they know how they are made?

Find out what the children's favourite potato or sandwich fillings are. Talk about any that the children have not tried. Read out your list of tasty fillings from the photocopiable page. Explain that together you are going to make a big plate full of tasty mini baked potatoes for everybody to try.

Show the children your new potatoes and ask the children to take turns to scrub and then dry a few. Together, prick the skins of the potatoes carefully and place them in a baking tin. Drizzle over a little oil and ask for help to roll the potatoes around in the tin to coat them with oil.

Place the potatoes in a pre-heated oven at 200°C/400°F/gas mark 6 for around 20 minutes until cooked.

Ask the children to wash their hands and help you to prepare a selection of fillings which can be placed in dishes ready to serve.

When the potatoes are cooked an adult should split them open and the children can spoon in the different fillings, taking care not to touch the hot potatoes. When they have cooled a little, arrange them on large plates and encourage the children to try some new, as well as their favourite, tastes.

HOME LINKS
Copy photocopiable page 67 for the children to take home. For each child, tick the fillings that they have tried. Draw smiley faces next to the ones that they enjoyed.

Support and extension
Do any chopping or pricking for younger children. Invite older children to help you to write a recipe for cooking baked potatoes.

Further ideas
■ Set up your role-play area as a baked potato bar and serve the potatoes as part of imaginative play.
■ Make a bar chart showing the children's favourite potato fillings.

Mash, mix or chop?

What you need
Ingredients: 250g (8oz) trimmed green beans; 2 x 185g cans of tuna; 1 red pepper, sliced; 2 x 400g tins of flageolet beans; 6 tbsp olive oil; 2 tbs white wine vinegar; 1 crushed garlic clove; salt and pepper.
Equipment: saucepan; hob; large bowl; salad servers; whisk; knives; jug; spoons; small plastic pots with lids.

What to do
Ask the children to tell you any 'cooking' words that they know, such as 'mash', 'mix' and 'chop'. Tell them that you are going to mime a cooking action and that you would like them to work out what you are doing. Mime mixing, chopping or mashing for the children to guess. Now let the children take it in turns to mime a cooking action.

Explain that you would like their help to make a tuna and bean salad for them to take home. Tell them to listen out for any special cooking words that you use as you work together (such as 'flake', 'whisk', 'drain', 'pour' and 'toss'). Write down any that the children notice.

Make the salad together by cooking the green beans in boiling water for three minutes, then draining and cooling them before placing in a large bowl. Drain a tin of tuna, flake it into large chunks and add it to the bowl. Tip in the drained tins of flageolet beans and the slices of red pepper.

Now make the salad dressing by whisking together the olive oil, vinegar, garlic, salt and pepper. Pour the dressing over the salad and toss it with large salad servers. Divide the salad into the children's plastic pots and refrigerate to keep it fresh until home time.

Read back the list of cooking words. Repeat the miming game using some of the new words that the children have learned.

Support and extension
Concentrate on learning three cooking words with young children, choosing words that are easy to mime. Encourage older children to use their cooking vocabulary as they work.

Further idea
■ Write the cooking words on to large pieces of card and fix them to the wall above the 'cooker' in the home corner.

LEARNING OBJECTIVES
STEPPING STONE
Build up vocabulary that reflects the breadth of their experiences.

EARLY LEARNING GOAL
Extend their vocabulary, exploring the meanings and sounds of new words. (CLL)

GROUP SIZE
Up to four children.

HOME LINKS
Let the children take home their salads to share with their families.

Veggie pasta

What you need

Ingredients: 250g (8oz) dried pasta shapes; 90g (3oz) mangetout; 1 small red pepper, chopped); 12 cherry tomatoes, halved; 4 tbsp sweetcorn; a handful of broccoli florets; 3 tbsp mayonnaise.

Equipment: photocopiable sheet 'Five a day' on page 68; saucepan; hob; mixing bowl; serving bowls; spoons; sharp knife (adult use only); cooking scales; sieve or colander.

What to do

Teach the children the 'Five-a-day' song on photocopiable page 68. Sing it together several times.

Have a general discussion about the children's favourite fruit and vegetables and explain that it is important to try to eat five portions of different fruit and vegetables a day.

Tell the children that they will be making a pasta dish using five different fruits and vegetables. Show the children your prepared fruit and vegetables and ask them to identify any they can.

Weigh out the pasta together and place it in a pan of boiling water. Cook as per the packet instructions. During the last two to three minutes of cooking time, add the broccoli, pepper and mange tout. Drain when cooked, transfer to a large mixing bowl and leave to cool. Ask the children to add the sweetcorn, cherry tomatoes and mayonnaise and mix everything together thoroughly in the bowl.

Let the children serve the pasta in small bowls. Does each serving of the pasta contain all the five fruits and vegetables?

Support and extension

Help younger children to serve the food, encouraging them to use spoons rather than fingers! Let older children help you to chop and prepare the vegetables.

Further ideas

■ Let the children choose their five favourite vegetables to make a variation of this pasta dish.
■ Use cooking equipment such as wooden spoons, whisks and pans to make some percussion accompaniment to go with the song!

LEARNING OBJECTIVES

STEPPING STONE
Respond to simple instructions.

EARLY LEARNING GOAL
Listen with enjoyment and respond to stories, songs and other music, rhymes and poems and make up their own stories, songs, rhymes and poems. (CLL)

GROUP SIZE

The whole group for the song; small groups for the cooking activity.

HOME LINKS

Explain to parents and carers that the children have been learning about five portions of fruit and vegetables a day as part of a healthy diet. Suggest that the children find out what their parents' or carers' favourite fruit and vegetables are.

Cheesy vegetable tarts

What you need

Ingredients: ½ tomato, finely chopped; ½ small carrot, finely chopped; ½ small courgette, diced; 2 tbsp sweetcorn; 60g (2oz) tinned kidney beans, drained; 90g (3oz) cheddar cheese, grated; one sheet ready-rolled shortcrust pastry; small amount of cooking oil; oven.

Equipment: different-sized round pastry cutters; nine-hole bun tin; oven; knives; forks; bowls; rolling pins; cheese grater.

What to do

Lay out the sheet of pastry on a lightly floured surface and talk about its shape. Cut it into four equal pieces and decide what new shapes you have made.

Give each child a selection of round pastry cutters and allow them to cut out some shapes. Encourage them to name the shapes and compare the different sizes.

With the children's help baste the bun tin with a little oil. Talk about the shapes they notice. Compare the different-sized pastry circles with the size of the holes in the tin. Which size pastry circle will fit best?

Let the children re-roll the pastry, this time cutting out the most appropriate size of pastry circle. Press the pastry circles into the bun tin, prick with a fork and bake in a medium oven for about 15 minutes.

While the pastry is cooking ask the children to help you to mix the vegetables together. Then fill each cooked pastry case with the vegetable mixture and sprinkle the cheese on top. Take care that the children do not touch the hot bun tin. Bake the tarts in a medium oven for about ten minutes.

Support and extension

Provide two very different-sized pastry cutters for younger children to compare. Introduce the concept of tessellation to older children. Show them how the circle cutters leave pieces of pastry over, but how a square cutter could use all the pastry up!

Further ideas

■ Make biscuits using a range of different-shaped pastry cutters.
■ Look at a selection of fruit and vegetables, and describe and name their approximate shapes.

LEARNING OBJECTIVES

STEPPING STONE
Begin to use mathematical names for 'solid' 3-D shapes and 'flat' 2-D shapes and mathematical terms to describe shapes.

EARLY LEARNING GOAL
Use language such as 'circle' or 'bigger' to describe the shape and size of solids and flat shapes. (MD)

GROUP SIZE
Four children.

HOME LINKS
Ask parents and carers to help their children to describe and name the shapes of all the foods on their plates at mealtimes.

Strawberry fool

What you need
Ingredients: 19 fresh strawberries; 250ml (½pint) double cream, whipped;
60g (2oz) caster sugar.
Equipment: cooking scales; liquidiser/blender; whisk; jug; bowl; serving
dishes; spoons.

What to do
Ask the children to wash their
hands. Show them your bowl of
strawberries. Do they know what
the name of the fruit is? How
many strawberries do the children
think are in the bowl?

Pick out the strawberries from
the bowl, one by one, and ask the
children to count them with you.

Tell the children that you would
like their help to make delicious
strawberry fool puddings. Ask
one of them to count out four
strawberries from the pile to put
to one side. Explain that these will
be used to decorate the finished
desserts. Now ask the other three
children to each count out five
strawberries and liquidise them in
batches. Weigh out and add the
sugar to the mixture.

Ask the children to help you to whisk the cream to a thick, peaky, consistency.
Mix the puree and the whipped cream together and serve into dishes. Let
each child fill their own dish, counting out the number of spoonfuls. Garnish
with a fresh strawberry and enjoy!

Support and extension
Concentrate on counting up to three or four with younger children, show
them how to point to each strawberry as they say a number. Suggest that
older children divide the strawberries carefully between them before they
begin, making sure that each child has the same number. Are there any
strawberries left over?

Further ideas
■ Grow some strawberry plants in your outdoor setting. Count the number of
strawberries that grow on each plant.
■ Continue the counting work at snack time. For example, ask a child each
day to help you count out the number of biscuits or apple slices for each group
of children.

Dried fruit salad

What you need

Ingredients: ½ cup dried apricots, chopped; several glacé pineapple rings; ½ cup chopped dried apples; ½ cup raisins; 1 cup water; ½ cup orange juice; 2 tablespoons caster sugar; a fresh apricot; some fresh grapes; a fresh orange; a fresh apple; a fresh pineapple.

Equipment: citrus juicer; saucepan; hob; sharp knife (adult use only); large bowl; serving dishes; spoons; photocopiable sheet 'Fruit match' on page 69.

What to do

Let the children look at and taste each of the dried fruits. Explain that these fruits look quite different when they are fresh. Show the children your selection of fresh fruits. See if the children can match them to their dried counterparts? Cut the fresh fruit into pieces and invite the children to taste these, one by one. Can they match fresh and dried now?

Next, explain to the children that you are going to use the dried fruits to make a delicious dried fruit salad. Ask them to help you tip the dried fruits into the saucepan and mix them together with the sugar, water and orange

juice. Bring the fruits to the boil and simmer, covered, for about three minutes. Pour the mixture into a bowl and refrigerate until ready to serve. Let the children taste a small bowl full. Do the fruits taste different after they have been cooked?

Finally show the children how to make your own orange juice by cutting an orange in half and squeezing it on the juicer. Let the children taste it and compare it to the processed fruit juice. Which do they think tastes nicer?

Now give each child a copy of the photocopiable sheet and ask them to draw arrows to match the dried fruits with their fresh fruit counterparts.

Support and extension

Compare just two dried and fresh fruits with younger children. Let older children help you to chop some of the dried and fresh fruits.

Further idea

■ Make a fresh fruit salad. Ask the children to close their eyes as they taste the two dishes. Can they tell when they are eating dried or fresh fruits?

Creamy sweetcorn dip

What you need
Ingredients: 300g jar of sweetcorn relish; 300ml thick sour cream; handful each of cauliflower and broccoli florets; carrot, courgette and celery batons.
Equipment: vegetable peeler; knives; colander; spoons; mixing bowl; ramekins.

What to do
Talk to the children about healthy eating. Can they think of some foods that are good for them? Explain or remind them that it is important that we eat a good range of fresh fruits and vegetables each day. What are the children's favourite fruits and vegetables?

Show the children the prepared carrots, cauliflower and so on. Ask them if they know the names of the vegetables and if they have ever eaten them. Talk about how it is important to wash fresh fruits and vegetables before we eat them. Ask the children to help rinse the cut vegetables in a colander under running water. Explain that these vegetables can all be eaten raw and that they will be trying them with a creamy corn dip which they will be making.

Spoon the contents of the jar into a bowl with the sour cream and ask the children to take it in turns to mix the ingredients together. Allow each child to spoon a small amount into their own ramekin dish and ask them to select a few vegetables to use for dipping into the mixture. Explain how it is more hygienic to have individual dishes for dips, so that we are not transferring germs.

Which vegetables did the children enjoy dipping the most? Did they try any vegetables that were new to them or which they had not tried raw before?

Support and extension
Younger children may be more fussy about eating raw vegetables, so offer breadsticks, cheese, and apple slices instead. Encourage older children to make posters promoting healthy eating.

Further ideas
■ Look through some recipe books together, finding recipes that contain the children's favourite fruits and vegetables.
■ Blanch the vegetables by placing them in boiling water for a minute or two. Taste and compare the difference between the blanched and raw vegetables.

Pastry pears

What you need

Ingredients: sheet of ready-rolled puff pastry; 2 tsp caster sugar; pinch ground cinnamon; sprinkle of flour; 4 tinned pear halves, drained; 1 egg, lightly beaten; 2 tsp butter; 1 tbsp sultanas; 2 tsp brown sugar; 2 tsp desiccated coconut.

Equipment: knives; forks; round pastry cutter; pastry brush; spoons; small bowl; baking tray; oven.

What to do

Lay out the sheet of pastry on a clean, floured surface. Divide the sheet into four and give a piece to each child. Give each child a pastry cutter and ask them to cut out a round shape. Let them know they are going to make a treat to take home.

Help each child to place their pastry round onto a lightly greased baking tray. Give each child a knife and ask them to score gently a diamond pattern onto their piece of pastry. Brush the pastry pieces with egg, then sprinkle a little cinnamon and caster sugar over each one. Bake in a hot oven for about 15 minutes (until lightly browned).

While the pastry is cooking, let the children experiment with making shapes and patterns with the pastry trimmings. Suggest that they cut out leaf shapes and draw patterns on the leaves, for example.

Now ask the children to mix together the butter, brown sugar, coconut and sultanas. Give each child a pear half and ask them to fill the centre of the pear with a spoonful of the mixture. Carefully place the pears cut side down on the pastry rounds and bake until heated through (about five minutes).

Admire the finished pear pastries and encourage the children to talk about the tools and techniques they used to make their patterns.

Support and extension

Let younger children simply experiment with the marks they can make on the pastry. Challenge older children to make specific things from the pastry trimmings such as a veined leaf shape.

██████████████████████████████████████

Further ideas

■ Make other patterned pastry treats using the same techniques.
■ Look for examples of other types of food that have patterns drawn onto them, such as icing on cakes, fork patterns in mashed potato, malted milk biscuits and so on.

LEARNING OBJECTIVES

STEPPING STONE
Use simple tools to effect changes to the materials.

EARLY LEARNING GOAL
Handle tools, objects, construction and malleable materials safely and with increasing control. (PD)

GROUP SIZE
Four children.

HOME LINKS
Make these special pastries as a treat for an occasion such as Mother's Day. Help the children to make card baskets lined with a pretty serviette to place their pastry pear in and let them take them home.

Traffic-light fruit salad

What you need
Ingredients: mixture of red, green and yellow/orange fruits such as strawberries, raspberries, plum slices, kiwi slices, seedless red and green grapes, melon chunks, apricots, oranges, peach slices; 8 tbsp of orange juice; 4 tbsp strawberry jam.
Equipment: knives; chopping boards; large fruit bowl; small bowls; spoons; photocopiable sheet 'Traffic light fruits' on page 70.

What to do
Talk to the children about the colours in the traffic-light sequence. Can they name the colours? Do they know what they mean?

Now ask them to think of some fruits that come in the red, amber (or yellow/orange) and green colours. Make a list of their suggestions. Now show them the fruits you have chosen. Divide them into colour groups with the children's help. Ask the children to wash and help you prepare and select quantities of the fruits for a traffic light fruit salad.

Mix the fruits with the orange juice and jam, chill for a couple of hours before serving.

After the children have enjoyed their fruit salad give them each a copy of the photocopiable sheet to complete. They must identify the fruits and colour them in their appropriate 'traffic light' colours.

Support and extension
Younger children may need support to recognise the fruits on the activity page. Encourage older children to draw extra red, green or orange/yellow fruits on the back of the page.

Further ideas
■ Make traffic-light fruit tarts by popping the fruits in pastry cases and then covering them in confectioner's custard.
■ Make some food colour books together. Staple together a few pieces of sugar paper and add a coloured card cover. Fill the pages with drawings, paintings and cut out pictures of food in the same colour as the cover. For example, a red book might contain pictures of a tomato, a strawberry, a bottle of tomato sauce, a red pepper and a raspberry.

No-cook recipes

The recipes in this chapter have been chosen for the fact that they don't require a cooker. Through trying out these ideas the children will develop a range of techniques as well as an appreciation of shape, size, colour and texture, and an awareness of change.

Cottage cheese dip

What you need

Ingredients: 225g (8oz) cottage cheese; 4 tbsp mayonnaise; 4 tbsp snipped chives; 1 tbsp tomato puree; salt and pepper; breadsticks, crackers or pitta bread fingers for dipping.
Equipment: Sieve; wooden spoon; bowl; spoons; kitchen scissors (for use under adult supervision); ramekins.

What to do

Ask the children if they have ever tasted cottage cheese. Let them taste a spoonful now. How would they describe the texture and the taste? Is it hard or soft, smooth or lumpy (or both)?

Explain to the children that you will be making a tasty dip with the cottage cheese and some other ingredients. Show the equipment and ask the children if they have any ideas for how the dip could be made and how they might get rid of the lumpy texture of the cheese.

Place a sieve over a bowl and demonstrate how to use the back of a spoon to press out the lumps from the cottage cheese into the bowl below. Let the other children in the group take turns to do this.

Mix the 'pressed' cheese together with the chives, mayonnaise, tomato purée and salt and pepper.

Spoon the mixture into ramekins and encourage the children to try the new taste, dipping in breadsticks, pitta bread fingers or crackers.

Support and extension

Talk about other lumpy foods that young children have tried, such as rice pudding and porridge. Give two older children the task of snipping the chives into tiny pieces using kitchen scissors (make sure they are closely supervised).

Invite older children to talk about the change in texture from lumpy cottage cheese to smooth dip.

Further ideas

■ Compare a range of ready-made dips with different tastes and textures (such as lumpy salsa dip and smooth cream cheese dip).
■ Encourage the children to talk about the first time that they tasted some of their favourite or least favourite foods.

LEARNING OBJECTIVES
STEPPING STONE
Have a positive approach to new experiences.

EARLY LEARNING GOAL
Be confident to try new activities, initiate ideas and speak in a familiar group. (PSED)

GROUP SIZE
Up to four children.

HOME LINKS
Suggest that parents and carers show their children a selection of safe kitchen equipment, talking about the different jobs they can do with the objects.

Truly fruity ice-lollies

What you need
Ingredients: 120ml (4floz) tropical fruit juice; small banana; peach and an equal amount of mango.
Equipment: blender or food mixer; 4 ice-lolly moulds; sharp knife or vegetable peeler; bowl; sieve; spoons; freezer.

What to do
On a sunny day suggest to the children that they might like to cool down by making and eating their own fruity ice-lollies. Encourage the children to tell you about their favourite fruit flavours. Ask them to imagine how an ice-lolly might be made.

Tell the children that you would like them to work as a team to make the lollies. Explain how the fruit needs to be peeled and then chopped first. Let the children help with this, putting the prepared fruit into a bowl. Help them to press the mango pieces through a sieve to remove the fibres.

Place the prepared fruits and fruit juice into a blender or food mixer and blend together. Ask the children to work in pairs to spoon the blended mixture into the lolly moulds, with one child holding and the other spooning.

Put the lids on the moulds and place in the freezer for around two hours before enjoying them.

Support and extension
Younger children may need help to hold the moulds steady and upright as their partners are spooning in the mixture. Encourage older children to make up their own ice-lolly recipes using their favourite fruits and fruit juices.

Further ideas
■ Compile a recipe booklet of favourite ice-lolly mixtures.
■ Make fruity ice-cubes by pouring the same mixture into an ice-cube tray. Use the cubes to cool down cups of water on a hot day.
■ Have a 'blind' tasting session of a variety of the children's favourite fruits or fruit juices. Can they identify the tastes?

My own cereal

What you need
Ingredients: selection of fun-size packets of cereal; dried fruits such as raisins, apricots, dates, pineapple; fresh fruits such as banana and apple; milk to serve.
Equipment: cereal bowl for each child; bowls; children's knives and sharp knives; teaspoons.

What to do
Prepare and chop the fresh and dried fruits separately and put them into individual bowls. Let the children use plastic knives to cut the softer fruits, and cut up any more difficult ones yourself.

Talk about the different fruits. Ask the children if any of them eat fruit with their breakfast. Do any of them chop up fruit to add to their breakfast cereals?

Now look at the selection of small cereal packets. Help the children to identify each one. Invite them to take turns to tell the rest of the group about their favourite breakfast cereals. Is their favourite one there?

Explain to the children that you would like them to make their very own cereal by choosing a mixture of fruits and different cereal pieces. Encourage them to take it in turns to choose teaspoonfuls from the selections available. Invite them to talk about their choices.

Finish by helping the children pour milk on their cereal and letting them tuck in!

Support and extension
Remind younger children of the different tastes of the fruits and cereals as they choose them. Let them taste a sample of each choice before deciding whether to add some to their bowl. Suggest that older children write out a recipe showing all the ingredients of their home-made cereals.

Further ideas
■ Encourage the children to design packets for the children's newly invented breakfast cereals. Help the children to decide on a name for their cereal.
■ Find out what the most popular ingredient for the cereal mixtures is.

LEARNING OBJECTIVES
STEPPING STONE
Have emerging self-confidence to speak to others about wants and interests.

EARLY LEARNING GOAL
Interact with others, negotiating plans and activities and taking turns in conversation. (CLL)

GROUP SIZE
Up to six children.

HOME LINKS
Make sure that you have any information regarding food allergies before letting the children try a range of cereals (as some contain wheat products and nuts) or adding milk. Check the ingredients on the packets carefully to make sure that all the ingredients are safe for all the children.

Salmon pâté

What you need

Ingredients: 100–120g tin red salmon (boneless and skinless), drained; 60g soft/cream cheese; 4 tbsp mayonnaise; 2 tsp lemon juice; 40–50g butter, softened; French toast or pitta bread fingers to serve.

Equipment: food processor; mixing bowl; citrus juicer; knives; weighing scales; spoons; ramekins.

What to do

Tell the children that you would like their help to make a salmon pâté. Explain that in order to make it they will need to do things in the correct order. For example, the ingredients need to be weighed out before they can be combined.

Show the children your equipment and the ingredients. What things do they think need to be done and in what order? (They will need to weigh out the salmon, cream cheese and butter; juice the lemon; measure out the mayonnaise and chop the parsley. When all the ingredients are ready they can simply blend them all together in a food processor. Lastly they need to spoon out the mixture into small dishes ready to serve with pieces of bread or toast.)

Write down the children's suggested instructions and use them to refer to as you make the pâté together. As you follow the children's method carefully, decide whether the instructions are in the right order and if anything has been missed out.

Support and extension

Talk through the sequence step-by-step with younger children. Ask them obvious questions such as, 'Can we add the lemon juice before we squeeze it?' Invite older children to copy out the recipe instructions in their best writing.

Further ideas

■ Add extra mayonnaise to the mixture to transform it into a dip.
■ Look at some packaging for bought pâtés. What are the ingredients? Can the children imagine how these pâtés might be made?

LEARNING OBJECTIVES
STEPPING STONE
Begin to use talk instead of action to rehearse, reorder and reflect on past experience, linking significant events from own experience and from stories, paying attention to sequence and how events lead into one another.

EARLY LEARNING GOAL
Use talk to organise, sequence and clarify thinking, ideas, feelings and events. (CLL)

GROUP SIZE
Four children at a time.

HOME LINKS
Invite the parents and carers to come in and share the children's home-made pâtés. Encourage the children to explain how they made them.

Turkey and cream cheese rollers

What you need
Ingredients: 1 tortilla wrap per child; 3–4 slices wafer-thin turkey or chicken per child; thin slices of cheese (two per child); 1 tbsp of spreadable cheese per child; slices of tomato and cucumber; selection of different– shaped breads.
Equipment: spoons; knives; photocopiable sheet 'Food shapes' on page 71.

What to do
Talk about the children's favourite types of sandwich. Have they tried different kinds of bread as well as different fillings? Look at some different types of bread, discuss the shapes that they come in (for example, an oval pitta bread; a rectangular slice from a sandwich loaf; a circular tortilla wrap and so on).

Now give each child a tortilla wrap. Tell them that they will be making their own sandwich using this bread. What shape is it?

Ask them to spread their wrap with some cream cheese and then show them how to lay on slices of cold meat, cheese, tomato and cucumber.

Demonstrate how to roll the bread into a cylinder shape. Talk about the shape they have made. Now help the children to cut their roll into four smaller cylinders. Refer to the shapes and the change in size. Help them to understand that one long cylinder has made the four smaller ones.

After you have enjoyed eating the sandwiches, show the children an enlarged copy of the photocopiable sheet. Talk about the different foods that the children recognise. What shapes are they? What other shapes do the children think sandwiches can come in?

Support and extension
Concentrate on simple shape names such as 'circle' and 'square' with younger children. Encourage them to use words such as 'flat', 'big' and 'round' to describe shapes and sizes. Introduce three-dimensional shape names to older children and encourage them to use comparative vocabulary such as 'bigger'.

Further ideas
■ Cut out some food pictures from magazines and catalogues. Ask the children to sort them into groups of different shapes and sizes.
■ Continue to discuss the shapes of food at snack times. What shapes are the children's biscuits? What shapes have the bananas and apples been cut into?
■ Make some shape sandwiches using pastry cutters.

LEARNING OBJECTIVES
STEPPING STONE
Begin to talk about the shapes of everyday objects.

EARLY LEARNING GOAL
Use language such as 'circle' or 'bigger' to describe the shape and size of solids and flat shapes. (MD)

GROUP SIZE
Four children.

HOME LINKS
Encourage parents and carers to continue identifying food shapes at home.

Ham surprise!

LEARNING OBJECTIVES
STEPPING STONE
Count out up to six objects from a larger group.

EARLY LEARNING GOAL
Use developing mathematical ideas and methods to solve practical problems. (MD)

GROUP SIZE
Pairs.

What you need
Ingredients: 5 slices of sandwich ham; grated cheddar cheese; tinned pineapple chunks in fruit juice; diced apple.
Equipment: cheese grater; knives; vegetable peeler; sieve; bowls; cocktail sticks.

What to do
Invite the children to help you prepare the ingredients for a ham surprise. Explain that they will be rolling up fillings inside slices of ham to share with a partner.

Ask the children to help you drain the tin of pineapple chunks using a sieve, reserving the juice to use another time. Let them help you (under supervision) to grate the cheese and peel and chop the apple into little cubes.

Put all the ingredients into bowls and provide each child with a slice of ham. Ask them to sprinkle their ham with some grated cheese. Let them decide how much to add, using problem-solving skills to work out an appropriate amount that can be rolled up into the ham slice. Next ask them to count out a specified number of fruit pieces to place on top of the cheese. Make sure that their partner does not see which fruit they have chosen. Show them how to roll the ham slice carefully into a cylinder, securing it with a cocktail stick. Is the slice too full? What should they do if it is?

Ask the children to swap 'ham surprises' with each other. Can they taste which fruit their partner has added?

Support and extension
Younger children may need some help to count out the correct number of fruit pieces and will need assistance when rolling the ham slice. Ask older children to make several ham surprises, each one containing a different filling combination. Set challenges such as adding five pieces of fruit in three different ways (such as three apple, two pineapple; four apple, one pineapple; and two apple, three pineapple).

Further idea
■ Make an individual pizza by counting out different amounts of topping to add to the base, for example, five mushroom slices; two spoonfuls of sweetcorn; six pineapple chunks and so on.

HOME LINKS
Suggest to the children that they help their family to count out food at tea-time, such as the number of biscuits to go on a plate, or the number of potatoes to bake in the oven.

Banana snow cones

What you need
Ingredients: 5 small ripe bananas.
Equipment: masher or fork for each child; freezer; bowl; plastic container with a lid; ice-cream scoop or spoon; ice-cream cone for each child.

What to do
Show the children an unpeeled banana and let them handle it carefully. Do they know what it is? What does it feel and smell like? Now peel the banana and cut it into chunks. Let the children touch and taste the banana chunks, commenting on the texture and taste (for example, sweet).

Explain that they are going to help you to make some simple banana ice-cream, simply by mashing and then freezing the bananas. Give each child a banana, a bowl and a fork. Ask them to peel the banana, then mash it in the bowl. How would they describe its texture now?

Spoon all the mashed banana into a single plastic container and cover it. Freeze for two to three hours or until hard. Show the children the banana 'snow' and let them touch it lightly to see how the banana has changed again.

Let the mixture soften a little before scooping it onto ice-cream cones and enjoying. Which form of banana do the children like best?

Support and extension
Encourage younger children to describe the changes that they have noticed in simple terms, using words such as 'cold', 'hard' and 'mushy'. Suggest that older children draw a series of pictures that show the changes to the banana.

Further ideas
■ Investigate mashing and freezing some other soft fruits. How do these fruits change? Are any unsuitable for mashing or freezing? For example, strawberries are good for mashing and freezing, but grapes aren't!

■ Purée some strawberries to make a strawberry sauce for the banana snow cones. Ask the children to talk about how the strawberries have changed.

■ Set up your role-play area as an ice-cream parlour. Serve the cones to the children as part of imaginary play.

LEARNING OBJECTIVES
STEPPING STONE
Show an awareness of change.

EARLY LEARNING GOAL
Look closely at similarities, differences, patterns and change. (KUW)

GROUP SIZE
Four children at a time.

HOME LINKS
Encourage parents and carers to let their children prepare a banana snow cone at home for somebody that they live with.

Avocado dip

LEARNING OBJECTIVES

STEPPING STONE
Show curiosity, observe and manipulate objects.

EARLY LEARNING GOAL
Investigate objects and materials by using all of their senses as appropriate. (KUW)

GROUP SIZE
Up to four children.

What you need
Ingredients: 2 ripe avocados; 100g finely grated cheddar cheese; 2 skinned tomatoes (and 1 with skin on for comparison); 4 tsp natural yoghurt; carrot and celery sticks for dipping; breadsticks or pitta bread fingers.
Equipment: forks; potato masher; knives; mixing bowl; spoons and teaspoons; small bowls or ramekins; plates.

What to do
Show the children a whole avocado and allow them to feel it. Talk about the texture of the skin, how heavy it is and if it smells at all.

Now cut the avocado in half in front of the children. Are they surprised to see the stone? Take the stone out, give it a quick wipe and allow each child to handle it in turn. Ask questions such as: What shape is it? Is it rough or smooth? What can the children tell you about it?

Next peel off the skin and allow the children to touch the slippery flesh. Chop the avocado into pieces into the mixing bowl. Add the other avocado and let the children take it in turns to mash them together.

Show the whole tomato, then look at the ones that you have skinned. Chop the skinned tomatoes into tiny pieces and add them to the mixing bowl. Ask the children to mash the avocado and tomato together. Add the grated cheese, and yoghurt and ask the children to mix them all together to make a delicious avocado dip.

Serve by spooning the mixture into small dishes and arranging carrot and celery sticks and pieces of bread or breadsticks next to the dip on a plate.

HOME LINKS
Make sure that parents and carers are told about any new tastes that the children have tried. They may be pleased to hear that their child will experiment with new fruits and vegetables!

Support and extension
Help younger children to learn new words to describe the avocado. Introduce words such as 'slippery' and 'mushy'. Let older children cut up and explore the textures, colours and smells of a range of different fruits and vegetables. Ask them to report their findings to the rest of the group.

Further idea
■ Press cut-up fruits and vegetables into sponges soaked in paint to make some fun prints.

Strawberry and banana shake

What you need
Ingredients: 8–10 strawberries; 300g strawberry yoghurt; ½ pint milk; 2 bananas.
Equipment: forks; mixing bowl; food processor or blender; spoons; knives; large plastic tumblers; straws.

What to do
Tell the children that they will be making a delicious strawberry and banana milkshake. Ask them what other milkshakes they have tried. Which is their favourite? Give each child two or three strawberries to wash. Show them how to pull off the leaves, then ask them to take turns to mash their strawberries in the mixing bowl.

Next, give each child a piece of banana to slice and then mash into the strawberry mixture. Let each child spoon out some of the yoghurt into the bowl and take a turn at mixing it all together. Once all the fruit and yoghurt has been added, help the children to pour some milk carefully into the bowl, stirring it carefully together.

Pour the mixture into a blender or food processor and whizz it until smooth (add a little more milk if necessary to ensure it can be sucked up through a straw!). Pour the milkshake into tumblers, add straws and enjoy the delicious, nutritious drink.

Support and extension
Younger children may find it easier to mash the fruit with the back of a large spoon or a potato masher. Let older children pour out their own milkshakes.

Further ideas
■ Develop mashing skills by inviting the children to make some banana toast by carefully mashing a banana onto a slice of toast.
■ Find out about other foods that you can mash, such as potato, swede and avocado.
■ Use rolling pins to crush biscuits placed in plastic food bags. Use the crushed biscuit mixture as the base for a cheesecake pudding.

LEARNING OBJECTIVES
STEPPING STONE
Engage in activities requiring hand-eye coordination.

EARLY LEARNING GOAL
Handle tools, objects, construction and malleable materials safely and with increasing control. (PD)

GROUP SIZE
Four children.

HOME LINKS
Explain to parents and carers that you have been developing the children's hand-eye coordination skills by helping them to mash, mix and pour. Encourage them to provide opportunities at home for their children to continue using these skills.

Banana split

LEARNING OBJECTIVES
STEPPING STONE
Work creatively on a large or small scale.

EARLY LEARNING GOAL
Explore colour, texture, shape, form and space in two or three dimensions. (CD)

GROUP SIZE
Four children at a time.

What you need
Ingredients: banana for each child; tinned fruit cocktail in juice; kiwi fruit; cottage cheese with pineapple or peach (enough for 1 tbsp per child); seedless grapes; glacé cherries; pouring cream.
Equipment: knives; plates; chopping board; tablespoons; spoons; small bowls.

What to do
Explain to the children that you are going to help them to make an exciting, colourful and exotic banana split!

To start with, ask the children to help you prepare and sort all the different fruit fillings. Show them how to peel and slice a kiwi fruit and put it into a bowl; wash some grapes and cut them in half. Drain the fruit cocktail and put it in a bowl.

Now give each child a plate with a large spoonful of cottage cheese in the middle of it. Tell the children that you would like them to select a mixture of fruits to decorate the top of the pile. Encourage them to choose different colours, shapes and textures, talking about their choices as they work.

When they have a spectacular fruit and cheese 'centre', give them each a banana, sliced in half lengthways, and help them to carefully arrange the banana lengths in a sort of oval shape around the central fruit and cheese pile.

Make some final touches with extra pieces of fruit. Pour on a little wiggle of cream and enjoy the banana split creation!

Support and extension
Chop the fruits for younger children. Let older children decide how to arrange their banana splits – for example they may wish to place the bananas underneath the pile of fruit and cheese or they may wish to attempt sticking shorter lengths of bananas upright into the middle of their piles!

HOME LINKS
Ask the children to find out what their parents' or carers' favourite special puddings are.

Further ideas
■ Collect packaging from bought desserts and set up a role-play 'pudding shop'. Talk about the different desserts, encouraging the children to describe them. Which ones look delicious? Which look sweet and sticky? Are any gooey and chocolatey? Are any crunchy?
■ Make peach melbas in a similar way, substituting the banana lengths for peach halves.

Around the world

Children, these days, grow up sampling food from around the world on a regular basis. The recipes in this chapter will provide both new and familiar tastes, and will encourage the children to find out where some of their favourite foods originate.

Kolaches

What you need
Ingredients: 110g (4oz) cream cheese; 110g (4oz) butter; 225g (8oz) plain flour; jar of mixed fruit jam; small cup of water.
Equipment: mixing bowl; rolling pin; wooden spoon; teaspoons; blunt knives; pastry brush; baking trays; oven.

What to do
Ask the children to tell you about their favourite special foods. What special foods do their family eat at parties or for important occasions?

Tell the children that they will be making some sweet pastry treats called kolaches. Explain that these mini fruity parcels are enjoyed by children and their families in some countries in Central Europe. Perhaps ask the children if they have eaten kolaches at home.

Ask the children to help you to beat the cheese and butter together using a wooden spoon. Show them how to stir in the flour to make a dough. Leave the dough to chill in the fridge for at least three hours.

As you come to roll out the dough, preheat the oven to 220°C (gas mark 7) and grease the baking trays. Give each child a lump of the dough to roll out and show them how to use a blunt knife to cut out square shapes. (The dough should be enough for around 16 squares.)

Add a teaspoonful of jam to the middle of each square and use a damp pastry brush to wet the edges of each square. Now fold the corners of the square up to a point in the middle and pinch the edges together.

Bake the parcels for about 15 to 20 minutes.

Support and extension
Let younger children have fun rolling out the dough, but cut out the shapes for them. Challenge older children to make each of their squares the same size.

Further ideas
■ Bring in some Chinese fortune cookies for the children to try – they are a similar shape with a different kind of filling!
■ Make some more dough and use pastry cutters to make small pastry treats. Use shapes that symbolise aspects of the children's varied cultures such as Christmas trees, Star of David shapes and so on.

LEARNING OBJECTIVES
STEPPING STONE
Talk freely about their home and community.

EARLY LEARNING GOAL
Have a developing respect for their own cultures and beliefs and those of other people. (PSED)

GROUP SIZE
Four children at a time.

HOME LINKS
Let the children take home their kolaches to share. Encourage parents and carers to talk to their children about any cultural or family food traditions.

Biscuit nachos

What you need
Ingredients: 175g small savoury biscuits or tortilla chips; 200g guacomole; 100g tinned kidney beans, drained; 2 small tomatoes, chopped finely; 60–100g cheddar cheese, grated.
Equipment: large serving plate; mixing bowl; wooden spoon; sharp knife (adult use); spoons.

What to do
Talk with the children about times when we share our food – such as cutting and sharing a birthday cake or sharing a bag of crisps with a friend.

Tell them that you would like them to work together to make a tasty snack that you will all share from one big plate, inspired by the Mexican dish, nachos. Ask the children what things they need to consider about preparing and eating the dish? For example, making sure that they take turns to mix the ingredients; that they share the food equally; that everyone can reach the plate and so on.

Ask the children to help you lay out the biscuits in a ring around the edge of the plate. Explain that the dip will be heaped in the centre of the plate. Now ask the children to take turns to mix together the beans and tomatoes. Spoon them onto the plate and cover with the guacomole dip and finally the grated cheese.

Show the children how to dip the biscuits from the edge of the plate into the centre mixture. Encourage them to share and to think of each other, by not eating more than their share and by making sure that their friends can all reach easily.

Support and extension
Let younger children use spoons as well as the biscuits to scoop up the mixture. Encourage older children to help you to decide on the best arrangement of the ingredients on the plate.

Further ideas
■ Make a selection of different dips and snacks for the children to take it in turns to pass around at snack time.
■ Find out about other Mexican food such as enchiladas, burritos (see page 40) and chilli-con-carne.

Cheesy rarebit

What you need

Ingredients: 125g (4oz) mature cheddar cheese, grated; 125g (4oz) cream cheese; 1 tbsp butter; 1 tsp Worcestershire sauce; 1 tsp fresh chives, snipped; pinch of mild chilli powder; 4 thick slices of bread.

Equipment: mixing bowl; spoons; tsp; grill; knives; photocopiable sheet 'Welsh rarebit' on page 72; selection of cookery books and food packaging containing recipes and pictures of food from around the world; hole punch; ribbon; brightly coloured card folder; felt-tipped pens; paper; scissors; glue.

What to do

Show the children the recipe on the photocopiable page. Explain that the recipe is adapted from a traditional Welsh one and that you would like it to be the first one for a group *World Food Cookery Book* that you will make together.

Now show the children your other recipe books. Talk about any distinctive dishes from around the world (such as curry, spaghetti, chilli-con-carne and so on). What countries do the recipes come from? What foods have the children tried? Make a list of all the foods that the children recognise from the books. Repeat the discussion by looking at the food packaging you have brought in.

Now make the Welsh rarebit with small groups at a time, following the recipe on the photocopiable page. Slice the cooked rarebit into fingers and eat it straight away.

Ask one of the children to colour in the recipe on the photocopiable page. Hole-punch one side of the recipe and insert it in a brightly coloured folder using ribbon. Add a title such as *Our World Food Cookery Book* and invite the children to add illustrations of favourite foods from around the world.

Support and extension

Let younger children talk freely about any foods that they enjoy! Challenge older children to tell you the name of a food they have tasted that nobody else has mentioned yet.

Further ideas

■ Hold a world food festival, making a variety of dishes for the children and their parents to taste.
■ Make a visit to the local supermarket to investigate the range of foods from around the world. Read the labels to find out what the foods are called and where they are from.

LEARNING OBJECTIVES
STEPPING STONE
Build up vocabulary that reflects the breadth of their experiences.

EARLY LEARNING GOAL
Extend their vocabulary, exploring the meanings and sounds of new words. (CLL)

GROUP SIZE
Whole group for the discussion; small groups for the activity.

HOME LINKS
Ask parents and carers to supply any favourite simple recipes from around the world to include in your group recipe book.

French onion dip

What you need
Ingredients: packet of French onion soup mix; 160ml (¼pint) crème fraîche; selection of fresh vegetables suitable for dipping such as cauliflower and broccoli florets, carrots and baby sweetcorn.
Equipment: mixing bowl; serving bowl; spoons; large plate; vegetable steamer; sharp knife (adult use only).

What to do
Find out if the children know what a 'dip' is. What dips have they tried? Which are their favourites?

Explain that they are going to help you to make a French onion dip to enjoy with some tasty vegetable dippers.

Put the crème fraîche in the mixing bowl and then measure out a spoonful (depending on how strong you want the flavour) of the French onion soup mix to add to it. Ask the children to take turns to mix the ingredients together. As the children mix the dip use the opportunity to think together of some words that rhyme with 'dip' (such as 'lip', 'sip', 'tip', 'pip', 'ship', 'rip', 'chip' and so on). Write the rhyming words on a piece of paper or a board and read them through together.

Now chop the vegetables into strips ready to dip and steam them for a minute or two, to soften them a little.

Transfer the dip into a serving bowl and place it in the centre of your serving plate. Arrange the cooled vegetables around the bowl ready to share together.

After the children have enjoyed their snack, group them together and remind them of their list of rhyming words. Help them to make up some nonsense rhyming strings about the dip. For example, 'I got some dip on my lip – I tried to sip the dip!' or 'Don't put your chip in my dip!'

Support and extension
Help younger children to hear and enjoy the words that rhyme with 'dip'. Give older children a piece of paper with the letters '-ip' written several times in a column. Leave spaces for them to add letter sounds in front to make a string of rhyming words.

Further idea
■ Challenge the children to say a word that rhymes with *dip* each time they select a vegetable to dip into the French onion mixture!

Ciabatta pizza

What you need

Ingredients: 1 ciabatta loaf, split lengthways; 3 tbsp olive oil; small jar of tomato pasta sauce; 150g (5oz) sliced mozzarella cheese; 125g (4oz) sliced ham; 6 mushrooms, sliced thinly; half a red pepper, sliced; small tin of pineapple chunks in fruit juice, drained; button onion, sliced thinly.

Equipment: photocopiable sheet 'Pizza topping challenge' on page 73; sharp knives (for adult use); spoons; blunt knives; baking sheet; pastry brush; coloured pencils.

What to do

Preheat the oven to 190°C (gas mark 5). Tell the children that you would like them to help you to make some tasty Italian pizzas made from ciabatta bread.

Show the children the two halves of the bread and explain that the children will work in pairs to cover the bread with a tasty topping. Start by brushing the cut sides of the bread with olive oil and then spread three or four tablespoons of the pasta sauce on top. Now ask the children to add toppings from the selection available. In turn, invite them to add a specific number of each thing, such as, 'add three mushrooms'; 'two pieces of pineapple'; 'four slices of cheese' and 'two pieces of ham'.

Every now and then ask the children to stop and compare the two different pizzas. Which has the most mushrooms/ham/pineapple? Do they have the same amount of pepper slices? And so on.

Brush the finished pieces with a little more olive oil and place on the baking sheet. Cook for around 10 minutes, until the cheese is bubbling. Cut and share the pizza to eat straight away.

Support and extension

Limit the counting to below five for younger children. Ask older children to count the total number of topping pieces.

■■■■■■■■■■■■■■■■■■■■■■■■■■■■■■■■■■■

Further ideas

■ Try the activity on photocopiable page 73. The children must make as many different pizzas as they can by drawing on different quantities and combinations of food onto the pizza bases.
■ Make pretend pizzas from play dough. Ask the children to count out pretend play dough toppings.

French toast shapes

What you need
Ingredients: 3–4 slices of bread; 2 eggs, beaten; 2 tbsp milk; 30–40g (1–2oz) butter.
Equipment: variety of different-shaped biscuit cutters (such as hearts, stars, teddies, circles, squares and so on); whisk or fork; shallow dish; frying pan and hob; kitchen towel.

What to do
Show the children your selection of biscuit cutters and talk about the shapes together. As well as identifying the name of the shape or the object, encourage the children to describe each one, using words such as 'straight', 'curvy', 'round', 'pointy', and so on.

Ask each child to select a shape and then show them how to press it into the bread slices to cut out the shapes. Aim to fit two shapes onto each slice of bread.

Now ask the children to beat together the eggs and the milk. Pour the mixture into a shallow dish. Let each child dip their bread shape in the batter and fry the shapes in butter until golden brown.

Drain the shapes on a piece of kitchen towel to remove the excess fat before eating and enjoying.

Support and extension
Help younger children to develop the appropriate vocabulary to describe the shapes. Under close supervision, let older children use a knife to cut out some shapes of their own from the bread. Suggest that they make, for example, three different-sized triangles or three different-sized squares.

Further ideas
■ Compare the French toast shapes to other objects in your group's environment. What objects are similar in shape to the ones that the children have made?
■ Use the cutters to make some shape sandwiches for snack time.

Hummus

What you need

Ingredients: 400g tin of chickpeas, drained (choose the no added salt and sugar variety); 1 tbsp olive oil; 2 tbsp tahini; 1 dessert spoon of freshly squeezed lemon juice; 1 tbsp low fat natural yoghurt; 1 crushed clove of garlic; selection of raw vegetables for chopping.

Equipment: photocopiable sheet 'Technology cards' on page 74; garlic press; juicer; blender; food mixer with a vegetable chopping disc/attachment; spoons; serving bowl; serving plate.

What to do

Lay out all the equipment that you have used or will be using on a table. Show the children each thing and talk about what it will be used for. Do the children know what a blender and food mixer can do? Make sure you remind the children about the dangers of kitchen and electrical equipment. Stress that they must not touch objects like this unless they are closely supervised by an adult.

Explain to the children that you would like them to help you to make a dip called hummus. Invite them to put all the ingredients (except the vegetables) together into the blender. Let each child have a turn at pushing the buttons to blend the ingredients. When the mixture is smooth, transfer it to a serving bowl and keep it covered until the vegetables are ready.

Next, show the children the special attachment for the food mixer and demonstrate how it works. Under close supervision, let the children take turns to drop a vegetable into the compartment and then press the button to chop it.

Arrange the chopped vegetables on a serving plate around the bowl of hummus. It's now ready to enjoy!

Support and extension

Work closely with pairs of younger children. Extend the activity by demonstrating some other things that a food mixer can do.

Further ideas

■ Give the children the cards from photocopiable page 74. Talk about the pictures of kitchen technology (such as a cooker, microwave, mixer and so on). What jobs do the machines do? Which ones have the children seen their parents using? Older children could attempt to label the objects.

■ Ask the children to colour and cut out the pictures on the photocopiable sheet, then stick them on a separate piece of paper in an arrangement to make a kitchen picture.

LEARNING OBJECTIVES

STEPPING STONE
Know how to operate simple equipment.

EARLY LEARNING GOAL
Find out about and identify uses of everyday technology. (KUW)

GROUP SIZE
Two to four children.

HOME LINKS
Ask parents and carers to talk to their children about any kitchen equipment they have at home. Make sure that important safety messages are also conveyed.

Pizza dough

What you need

Ingredients: 350g (12oz) strong plain flour; 1 tsp salt; 1 tsp easy blend yeast; 200ml (7floz) warm water; 1 tbsp olive oil; margarine for greasing; pizza topping such as tomato-based pasta sauce, grated cheese, chopped ham and sliced mushrooms.

Equipment: baking sheet about 14 x 10in (35 x 25cm); mixing bowl; sieve; wooden spoon; large bowl; paper towel; plastic food wrap; oven.

What to do

Tell the children that you would like them to help you to make a pizza base and talk about the ingredients that they will be using.

Open the easy blend yeast packet to let the air get to it while together, you sieve the flour and salt into a mixing bowl. Add the oil, yeast and warm water and take turns with the children to stir well until you get a soft dough that doesn't stick to the sides of the bowl.

Ask the children to wash their hands then take turns to knead the dough on a surface sprinkled with flour. Show the children some kneading techniques, such as using the heels of their hands to push the dough away from them and folding the dough and turning it round. Encourage the children to keep kneading until the dough is smooth and stretchy.

Put the dough inside a large greased bowl and cover the top with plastic wrap. Leave it in a warm place for about 45 minutes until the dough is about twice the size. Preheat the oven to 220°C (gas mark 7). Quickly knead the risen dough to burst the air bubbles inside it.

Now press the dough into the required shape on your greased baking sheet. Pinch up the edges ready for adding a topping of your choice. Then cook for around 20 minutes.

Support and extension

Prepare the dough in advance for younger children and simply allow them some time to knead and manipulate the dough to make a pizza base. Encourage older children to explore the dough further, trying out a range of tools to make marks on or cut the dough.

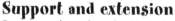

Further idea

■ Make different shapes from the dough, such as circles, stars or hearts.

LEARNING OBJECTIVES
STEPPING STONE
Explore malleable materials.

EARLY LEARNING GOAL
Handle tools, objects, construction and malleable materials safely and with increasing control.

GROUP SIZE
Four children.

HOME LINKS
Ask the children to talk about any baking they have done at home, did any of the recipes require rolling out dough or pastry?

Traditional English teabread

What you need
Ingredients: 250g (8oz) wholemeal self-raising flour; pinch of salt; 2 eggs; ½ tsp ground mixed spice; 125g (4oz) light muscovado sugar; 90g (3oz) butter or margarine; 120ml (4 floz) milk; 30g (1oz) chopped dates; 30g (1oz) dried, chopped apricots; 30g (1oz) sultanas; vegetable oil for greasing.
Equipment: 1kg (2lb) loaf tin; greaseproof paper; sieve; wooden spoon; mixing bowl; jug; whisk or fork; a skewer; oven; cooling rack; serving plate; *The Tiger Who Came to Tea* by Judith Kerr (Picture Lions); your usual home corner set up for a tea party.

What to do
Read the story *The Tiger Who Came to Tea* to the children. Talk about all the different foods that the tiger ate.

Show the children the home corner, all set up for a tea party. Tell them that you would like their help in making some traditional English teabread to eat at the tea party.

Work with small groups at a time. Grease and line your loaf tin and preheat the oven to 160°C (gas mark 3). Ask the children to help you to sieve the flour, salt and mixed spice into a mixing bowl. Stir in the sugar, then rub in the butter using fingertips until the mixture looks like breadcrumbs. Beat together the egg and milk and add them to the bowl with all the dried fruits. Mix well before turning into the loaf tin and baking for around one hour, until risen and golden brown (check with a skewer to see if it is cooked through). Cool in the tin for ten minutes then turn out onto a cooling rack.

Cut the cake into slices and butter it. Lay the pieces on an elegant dish and serve it in the home corner.

Encourage the children to role-play a tea party in the home corner. Suggest some different scenarios for them to act out.

Support and extension
Younger children will need to be reminded of the story, so go into role with them. Challenge older children to role-play a different ending to the story.

Further idea
■ Have a group tea-party, asking the children to bring in their favourite tea-time dish to share.

Tharwala dahi

What you need
Ingredients: 400g low-fat set natural yoghurt; water; ½ cucumber, peeled and grated; ½ onion, grated; 1 green chilli, finely chopped; ½ tsp salt; 1 tsp garam masala; ½ tsp red chilli powder; 1 naan bread.
Equipment: sharp knife and chopping board (adult use only); bowls; mixing bowl; serving bowl; spoons; tea towel.

What to do
Tell the children that they will be making a traditional Asian dish that is usually served as an accompaniment to meat dishes. It can also be used as a topping for baked potatoes or as a spicy but cool dip.

Tell the children that you would like them to explore all the different textures of the ingredients as well as the taste of this dish. Start by asking them to squeeze the excess water from the grated onion and cucumber using a clean tea towel. Ask them what it felt like before and after the water had been squeezed out. Next let them taste a small spoonful of the yoghurt. Encourage them to use words such as 'smooth' and 'gooey' to describe it.

Now make the tharwala dahi by mixing water with the yoghurt to create a runny texture. Add the cucumber, onion, chilli and salt and stir well. How has the texture changed? How would the children describe the yoghurt now? (For example, 'lumpy', 'rough', 'chunky'.)

Pour the mixture into a serving dish and sprinkle over the garam masala to decorate. Slice the naan bread into fingers for dipping into the delicious mixture.

Support and extension
Support any children who are unwilling to try the new taste by letting them taste just the yoghurt or cucumber, which will probably be more familiar to them. Extend the activity by making a list of the words that the children use to describe the ingredients and dip. Can the children tell you which words refer to which ingredients/stage of the recipe?

Further ideas
■ Compare the taste of tharwala dahi with some shop bought tzatziki (a traditional Greek dish using similar ingredients). Are the textures the same?
■ Grate some other vegetables such as carrot and potato. Feel the textures of them. Is there much water in them when they are squeezed?

Nutritious snacks

Children love to snack, and most young children need to eat regularly to compensate for the enormous amounts of energy that they expend. This chapter shows that snacking need not be a bad habit, and can be a healthy way to eat.

Pizza fingers

What you need
Ingredients: large focaccia bread; jar of tomato pasta sauce; tomato slices; grated cheese; mushroom slices; tin of pineapple chunks, drained; chopped ham; red or yellow pepper, chopped; cooking oil.
Equipment: oven tray; sharp bread knife (adult use only); knives; bowls; spoons; oven; baking parchment and pencil.

What to do
Preheat the oven to a moderate temperature (around 170°C, gas mark 4). Oil your baking tray.

Cut the focaccia bread in half horizontally and then into fingers. Give each child two pieces and ask them to spread the pieces with some pasta sauce, taken from the jar.

Now show them all the different toppings you have prepared and placed into bowls. Talk about each one and ask the children to tell you about their favourite pizza toppings. Tell them that they can choose the toppings they place on their pizza fingers. Challenge them to make the two pizzas different in some way. They may, for example, choose the same toppings but arrange them in different patterns; or they may make one ham and pineapple finger and one cheese and tomato finger.

As the children work, encourage them to talk about what they are doing. What patterns are they making? Which pizza finger will they eat first?

When the children are happy with their toppings ask them to place their pizzas on the oiled baking tray (you may wish to write their names on a piece of baking parchment next to their pizza fingers so as to avoid confusion later!). Bake for around 10 to 12 minutes, until lightly browned.

Support and extension
Invite older children to help you to prepare and select the toppings to use. Younger children may need help to spread the pasta sauce onto the bread.

Further idea
■ Cut out small circles of bread and design pizza faces to bake, using the different toppings (grated cheese hair, a pineapple nose and so on!).

LEARNING OBJECTIVES
STEPPING STONE
Show increasing independence in selecting and carrying out activities.

EARLY LEARNING GOAL
Be confident to try new activities, initiate ideas and speak in a familiar group. (PSED)

GROUP SIZE
Up to four children at a time.

HOME LINKS
Ask the children to bring in some pizza packaging from home. Talk about all the different toppings.

Potato skins

What you need

Ingredients: 4 medium potatoes; sunflower oil; mayonnaise; tomato ketchup.

Equipment: fork; potato scrubber; sharp knife (adult use only); spoon; baking sheet; mixing bowl; pastry brush; spoons; plate and small bowl for the potato skins and dip.

What to do

Remind the children about the importance of washing hands before we handle food. Explain that we should also make sure that the surfaces and cooking utensils we use are clean. Enlist the children's help to wipe down the surfaces and check the equipment.

Now tell them that it is important that we wash fruits and vegetables before we cook or eat them to remove any dirt or traces of chemicals from pesticides and so on.

Explain that you would like their help to make some delicious potato skins. Start by giving each child a potato to wash and scrub. When it is really clean, ask them to prick the potato with a fork and rub it with some oil before an adult places them on a shelf in a preheated oven (200°C, gas mark 6).

Bake the scrubbed potatoes for around an hour and a quarter (until soft inside). Leave them to cool before cutting in half and scooping out the flesh with a spoon. Cut each half into about three strips. Once more remind the

children of hygiene and, after they have washed their hands, ask them to brush the potato strips on each side with oil before placing them on a baking tray. Return to the oven for around 15 minutes (until crisp).

Arrange the potato skins on a plate with a simple dip such as equal quantities of mayonnaise and tomato ketchup mixed together.

Remind the children of the hygienic way to dip their potato skins. Make sure that they understand that they must not lick the skins and then dip them!

Support and extension

Supervise younger children when they are washing their hands. Let older children help to scoop out the potato flesh.

Further idea

■ Talk about some other times when we need to make sure we have washed our hands.

Dippy delights

What you need

Ingredients: 225g tub of cream cheese; two tbsp mayonnaise; 225g (8oz) crème fraîche; pinch of salt and pepper (for the basic dip); for the added ingredients try a selection of the following: grated cheese, chopped chives, chopped tinned tomatoes, small tin of drained sweetcorn, small tin drained flaked tuna, mustard, chutney; pitta bread fingers, breadsticks and cheesy biscuits for dipping.

Equipment: photocopiable sheet 'My dip recipe' on page 75; mixing bowls; small bowls; plates; cheese grater; spoons; sharp knife (adult use); pencils; felt-tipped pens; card; paper.

What to do

Explain to the children that they will help you to make a large bowl full of a basic creamy dip that they will be adding some extra ingredients to.

Let the children help you to make the basic dip by mixing together the cream cheese, mayonnaise, crème fraîche and salt and pepper. Show the children your selection of other ingredients and ask them to choose one or two that they think will mix in nicely with the basic dip.

Give each child a small bowl and let them spoon out two to three tablespoons of the basic dip into it. Let them add their own extra ingredients.

Ask each child to make up a name for their dip. Provide them each with a label and suggest that they write the name of their dip onto it, scribing for them if necessary. Now give each child a recipe template and suggest that they draw a picture of their dip in the box provided. Ask them to try to write a list of ingredients underneath. Invite them to tell you how they made their dips and scribe some words for them underneath (in the 'What to do' section of the template).

Support and extension

Younger children will need to be closely supervised when adding their extra ingredients! They will also need help to write their list of ingredients. Encourage older children to have a go at writing their own 'What to do' section.

Further idea

■ Look at packaging for commercially made dips and ask the children to design their own packaging for their dips by drawing a picture to stick onto an empty box or carton.

LEARNING OBJECTIVES
STEPPING STONE
Use writing as a means of recording and communicating.

EARLY LEARNING GOAL
Attempt writing for different purposes, using features of different forms such as lists, stories and instructions. (CLL)

GROUP SIZE
Up to five children at a time.

HOME LINKS
Display the children's dips with their labels and invite parents and carers to come in and sample them when they come to pick up their child.

Chicken burritos

LEARNING OBJECTIVES

STEPPING STONE

Hear and say the initial sound in words and know which letters represent some of the sounds.

EARLY LEARNING GOAL

Link sounds to letters, naming and sounding the letters of the alphabet. (CLL)

GROUP SIZE

Six children.

What you need

Ingredients: 3 flour tortillas; 60ml mayonnaise; 60ml crème fraîche; 60g (2oz) lettuce, finely shredded; 2 medium tomatoes, chopped finely; 60g (2oz) grated cheese; 250g (7–8oz) cooked chicken, chopped.

Equipment: photocopiable sheet 'What begins with 'b'? on page 76; some foods beginning with the letter 'b'; mixing bowl; spoons; sharp knife (adult use); plates to serve; paper and pen; coloured pencils.

What to do

Show the children your selection of foods beginning with the letter 'b', such as biscuits, bread, bananas and buns. Emphasise the letter sound and ask the children to suggest any other 'b' words (food or otherwise) that they can think of.

Explain that they will be helping you to make some burritos. Show them the ingredients and ask the children to take it in turns to mix the chicken, mayonnaise and crème fraîche together.

Give each pair of children a tortilla and ask them to lay it out flat. Invite them to spoon out some tomato, lettuce and cheese onto the tortilla. Divide the chicken mixture between the three tortillas and ask the children to spread it out. Show them how to roll up the tortilla securely, enclosing the filling. Tell the children that these rolls are called 'burritos'! Cut them in half and let the children enjoy them.

Finish by giving each child a copy of the photocopiable sheet. Ask them to identify and colour appropriately all the foods that begin with 'b'.

Support and extension

Younger children will need support to complete the sheet. Suggest that older children have a try at labelling each picture with its 'b' word.

Further ideas

■ Start a food alphabet list with the children, thinking of a food or drink beginning with each letter of the alphabet.
■ Try out some other recipes beginning with the letter 'b' such as burgers, blancmange or banana cake.

HOME LINKS

Encourage the children to choose a letter from the alphabet and look for food beginning with that letter at home. Suggest to parents and carers that they help their child to write a list of the foods that they found beginning with their chosen letter.

Cheese savouries

What you need
Ingredients: (to make 16 balls) 4 cream crackers; 120g (4oz) cream cheese; 2 tsp tomato ketchup; 2 small bags ready salted or cheese and onion crisps.
Equipment: plastic food bag; rolling pin; mixing bowl; wooden or plastic mixing spoons; 16 paper cake cases.

What to do
Show the children the paper cake cases and tell them that they will be helping you to make some savoury cheese balls to go into them. Challenge the children to share out the number of cake cases equally. Has everyone got the same number of cases? Count and check together, deciding what to do if the cases are not evenly divided.

Put the crackers in a plastic food bag and lay it on a clean work surface. Let the children take it in turns to use a rolling pin to gently crush the crackers until they are all in crumbs.

Combine the cream cheese and crushed crackers in a mixing bowl. Add the tomato ketchup and stir together.

Now crush the crisps inside their packets and shake them into a large bowl. Divide the cheese mixture evenly between the four children and ask them to make cheese balls from it by taking a piece and rolling it in the palm of their (clean) hands. Tell them that they need to make enough balls to fill their cake cases. Once they are satisfied that they have the corresponding number of balls, let them scatter a small amount of the crushed crisps onto the work surface to roll their cheese balls into. Place the crispy-coated cheese savouries in the cake cases.

Support and extension
Share out the cake cases for younger children and tell them the number of balls they need to make. Encourage them to count out the number of cake cases and balls as they work. Ask older children to count the total number of cheese savouries.

Further idea
■ Enjoy the cheese savouries at snack time. Continue the counting theme by asking the children to place one cheese savoury and three or four grapes on each plate. Can they check if all the children have got a plate and the right number of goodies?

LEARNING OBJECTIVES
STEPPING STONE
Use some number names accurately in play.

EARLY LEARNING GOAL
Say and use number names in order in familiar contexts. (MD)

GROUP SIZE
Four children.

HOME LINKS
Ask parents and carers to encourage their children's counting skills at home, for example by counting out the correct number of spoons when laying the table.

Mini salmon quiches

What you need

Ingredients: sheet ready-rolled shortcrust pastry; 105g tin red salmon (the skinless and boneless variety), drained and flaked; 125ml milk; 1 egg; butter for greasing.

Equipment: nine hole bun tin; round pastry cutters in three different sizes; pastry knife (adult use); rolling pins; mixing bowl and spoon; hand whisk or fork; small jug; oven.

What to do

Talk to the children about the ingredients and equipment you will be using for this activity. What shapes can they see in the equipment? Tell them that they will be using the circular pastry cutters to make some mini salmon quiches.

Cut the pastry into three pieces and give a piece to each child. Show them the bun tin and explain that they need to cut out three circle shapes each to go into the tin. Which cutter do they think will make pastry circles that will fit the tin? Let the children experiment with the different-sized pastry cutters to find out. Encourage them to use their initiative to re-roll the pastry to create the right shape needed to cut out their next circle.

Show the children how to press the cut-out pastry circles gently into the greased holes in the bun tin. Now combine the cheese and salmon and divide the mixture evenly between the pastry cases. Whisk the egg and milk together and pour the mixture over each salmon filled pastry case, just enough to cover the filling. Bake in a moderately hot oven (around 180°C, gas mark 5) for about 20 minutes (until filling is set). Let the quiches cool for a few minutes before taking them out of the bun tin.

Support and extension

Younger children will need help to re-roll the pastry. Encourage older children to make some different shapes from all the pastry scraps.

Further idea

■ Use sheets of pastry for some estimating work. Give the children different-sized pieces of pastry and ask them to guess, and then investigate how many of a specific shape they will be able to cut out from the pastry.

Savoury muffins

What you need

Ingredients: 300g self-raising flour; 60g ham, finely chopped; 80g cheddar cheese; 25g button mushrooms; 1 small red pepper; 1 tbsp fresh parsley; 130g butter; 250ml milk; 1 egg.

Equipment: photocopiable sheet 'Muffin mix up' on page 77; cheese grater; saucepan; wooden spoon; mixing bowl; three, 12-hole small muffin pans (40ml capacity); saucepan; cooker; wire racks; colouring materials; scissors; glue; paper.

What to do

Show the children all the ingredients before they have been chopped, grated, mixed or melted and talk about their appearance and texture. With the children's help, prepare the ingredients – finely chop the pepper, ham, mushrooms and parsley (an adult should melt the butter in a saucepan on the hob); beat the egg and grate the cheese. Talk about the difference in the appearance of the ingredients before and after preparation.

Now combine the flour, ham, cheese, mushrooms, pepper and parsley in a large bowl. Stir in the butter, milk and egg, taking care not to overmix. Once more, look at the appearance of all the ingredients now that they are combined. Ask the children to describe what they can see.

Help the children to divide the mixture evenly into the pan holes (it should make around 30 muffins). Bake in a preheated oven (180°C, Gas mark 5) for around 15 to 20 minutes. How has the mixture changed? Leave the muffins to cool in the tin for a few minutes before turning onto wire racks to cool.

Give each child a copy of the photocopiable sheet, showing the various stages in the sequence of muffin making. Ask the children to talk about the pictures, cut them out, and then decide the correct order, pasting them in sequence on a separate sheet of paper.

Support and extension

Give younger children lots of support to interpret and then sequence the pictures from the sheet. Help older children to make a zig-zag recipe book from the pictures. Encourage them to write a caption for each stage of the process.

Further ideas

■ Buy or make a selection of different flavoured muffins (sweet and savoury). Have a muffin tasting session. Can the children identify the different tastes? Which do they prefer?

■ Experiment with different ways of cooking eggs. Look at a raw egg and explore how eggs change when scrambled, fried, poached or boiled.

LEARNING OBJECTIVES
STEPPING STONE
Describe simple features of objects and events.

EARLY LEARNING GOAL
Investigate objects and materials by using all of their senses as appropriate. (KUW)

GROUP SIZE
Up to four children.

HOME LINKS
Encourage parents and carers to talk about the order of regular routines with their children.

Mini pitta pockets

What you need
Ingredients: mini pitta breads (enough for two to three per child); selection of healthy sandwich fillings, such as those listed on the photocopiable sheet 'Parcel fillings' on page 67.
Equipment: food magazines and food adverts showing some healthy and some 'junk' foods; mixing bowls; small bowls; mixing spoons; spoons; knives; plates.

What to do
Let the children look at your selection of food magazines and adverts. Encourage them to talk about the different foods, then steer the conversation towards which foods they consider are healthy and which they think are not so good for them. Talk to them about how we should eat a range of fruit and vegetables a day, and how we should limit our intake of fat, sugar and salt.

Explain to the children that you would like their help to make some tasty pitta pockets by filling mini pitta breads with some healthy fillings. Help the children to mix together the different fillings, such as tuna and chopped cucumber; egg, cress and mayonnaise and so on. Let the children choose their favourites and fill two to three mini pitta breads (sliced open).

Arrange the pitta breads on plates and encourage the children to try each other's creations!

Support and extension
Help younger children to begin to categorise some common foods into sets of sugary foods, fruits, vegetables and so on.

Further ideas
■ Make some healthy food scrapbooks by cutting out and sticking pictures of healthy food onto sheets of sugar paper which can be stapled or tied together.
■ Order some healthy living posters from your local health education authority. Display them above an interest table with the children's scrapbooks, books about fruits and vegetables and healthy food packaging.

Crunchy celery canoes

What you need
Ingredients: celery stick for each child; healthy fillings such as hummus, cottage cheese, egg mayonnaise, cream cheese with a sprinkle of raisins or pineapple chunks, guacamole (see photocopiable sheet 'Parcel fillings' on page 67 for more suggestions).
Equipment: large open space; pictures of different kinds of boats from sailing boats, cruise ships and ferries to canoes; spoons; sharp knife (adult use); knives for spreading.

What to do
Go to a large space with the children and ask them to think of all the different boats that they can, such as sailing boats, ferries, canoes, rowing boats and longboats. Show your pictures of different kinds of boats and discuss what they look like – some are big and bulky and move quite slowly; others are tall and elegant and race along in the wind.

Choose one type of boat at a time and ask the children to think about what the boat looks like and how it moves. Give them some ideas and let them copy your movements first, until they gain the confidence to try their own ideas. Try racing along like sailing boats in the wind, jumping waves and spinning round in storms or floating gently in the breeze during calm periods.

Back in the work area, tell the children that they are now going to make their own boat – a canoe made from celery which they can fill with a tasty mixture, eat and enjoy!

Wash and trim the celery and cut it into two or three equal pieces. Let the children choose what to fill their celery canoes with, from the selection available. Help them to fill the hollow, spreading it out with a blunt knife or the back of a spoon. Relax and enjoy them after all your hard work!

Support and extension
Concentrate on just two different types of contrasting boat with younger children. Encourage older children to think up their own movements. Invite individuals to demonstrate their ideas for others to copy.

Further idea
■ Use boat-shaped pastry cutters to make some boat sandwiches. Add paper sails by piercing triangle-shaped pieces of coloured paper with cocktail sticks to insert into the middle of the sandwiches

LEARNING OBJECTIVES
STEPPING STONE
Experiment with different ways of moving.

EARLY LEARNING GOAL
Move with confidence, imagination and in safety. (PD)

GROUP SIZE
Any size.

HOME LINKS
Ask the children to tell you about any boat journeys they have been on with their families.

Tasty bracelets

What you need
Ingredients: a selection of colourful healthy foods (as well as a few treat foods) suitable for threading or piercing with a blunt needle – ideas include dried apple rings; hoop-shaped crisps, cereals and sweets; pretzels; grapes; cucumber chunks; miniature cheeses; coconut ring biscuits.
Equipment: blunt-ended darning needles (cleaned by rinsing with boiling water); strong, clean thread or cord; bowls; spoons.

What to do
Make up an edible tasty bracelet before the activity and show it to the children. Place each different food in its own bowl in the middle of a table, ready for the children to select from. Talk about the different foods you have chosen for your bracelet. Comment on their sizes and colours as well as tastes, and draw the children's attention to any patterns that you have created.

Now tell the children that they will be making their own tasty bracelets using the various foods. Show them the selection of edible 'beads' you have prepared, making sure that the children know what each food is, allowing them to taste any that they have not tried before.

Give each child a threaded needle, with a knot at the end. Explain that they may add anything they choose to their bracelet. Encourage them to think about making their bracelets look appealing, as well as making them taste good. Draw their attention to the shapes and colours of the foods. Which colours look good together; which shapes sit nicely next to each other?

Let the children thread their bracelets and invite them to talk about their choices as they work. When all the children are happy with their creations spend some time admiring each other's work, talking about the taste and the appearance of the children's designs.

Finally relax and let the children enjoy the fruits of their work!

Support and extension
Younger children will enjoy practising their threading skills but will need extra help to pierce the foods that need to have holes added. Challenge older children to theme their bracelet by adding food in a repeating pattern of their choice, or by sticking to one colour or size.

Further idea
■ Thread multi-coloured pasta quills or macaroni onto wool or cord to make necklaces and bracelets.

Festivals and celebrations

The recipes in this chapter will put you in the mood for celebrating festivals such as Easter and the Chinese Moon festival as well as providing some tasty suggestions for general party and celebratory food and drink.

Yuebing (moon cakes)

What you need
Ingredients: (makes 20 cakes) 500g self-raising flour; 3 eggs; 3 tbsp vegetable oil; 100g sugar; 500g ready-to-eat dried figs; 20 ready-to-eat dried apricots; 1 egg yolk.
Equipment: large mixing bowl; wooden spoon; chopping knife (adult use only); food processor; 2 baking trays; fork; small bowl; pastry brush; oven.

What to do
Talk to the children about the Chinese Moon Festival, explaining that it is a celebration of the brightest and fullest moon of the year (the harvest moon). It takes place in mid autumn. Explain that the festival is a big holiday with family reunions, moon-gazing activities, and feasting on 'moon cakes' or *yuebing*, which are round pastries filled with fruits.

Ask the children to help you to make the moon cakes. Mix the flour, oil, eggs, sugar and water together in a bowl to make pastry. Let the pastry rest in the refrigerator for about half an hour.

Cut the figs into small pieces, then purée them in a food processor. Ask the children to wrap the apricots (five each) in the fig purée, by rolling the apricots in the fig mixture to make a small ball. Divide the pastry into 20 equal portions and then help the children to flatten the portions into circles (around 10cm in diameter). Wrap each pastry circle around a ball of fig purée and press the edges of the pastry together to make a sort of muffin shape. Turn the cakes over so that the sealed sides are underneath and then place them on a greased baking tray. Let the children prick the cakes with a fork. Brush the cakes with beaten egg yolk and bake them in an oven pre-heated to 200°C (gas mark 6) for about 30 minutes – until golden brown.

Support and extension
Let younger children each make one or two cakes only and support them at each stage of the process. Encourage older children to talk about other festivals that they celebrate at home.

Further idea
■ Hold a Chinese Moon Festival party with lion dancing, traditional music and feasting on moon cakes.

Crunchy nests

What you need

Ingredients: (for 8 nests) 2 squares of wheat cereal; 10–12 squares of chocolate; 24 small sugar-coated chocolate eggs; 2 tbsp raisins.
Equipment: saucepan of water; hob; glass bowl; wooden spoon; large plastic food bag; rolling pin; mixing bowl; spoons; 8 paper cake cases.

What to do

Talk about the festival of Easter with the children. What traditions are they aware of? Explain that eggs are a symbol of new life and beginnings, symbolic of Easter and of Spring, the season in which the festival occurs.

Tell the children that they will each take it in turns to make some Easter egg nests. Explain that you would like them to be as considerate as possible of the other children in their group, as well as the children that will do the activity later. For example, they must take it in turns to stir the mixture and share it evenly. They must clear up any mess they have made ready for the next group's turn, such as helping to wash up, clean surfaces and sweep up crumbs!

With these thoughts in mind, help the children to make their Easter nests. Melt the chocolate in a bowl over a saucepan of hot water. Place the wheat cereal into a large plastic bag and ask the children to gently crush them with a rolling pin.

Remove the chocolate from the heat and take turns with the children to mix the chocolate, crushed peices of wheat cereal and raisins together. When the mixture is all coated in chocolate, spoon out the mixture evenly between the cake cases. Ask the children to press down a little well in the centre of each nest and then count out and place three chocolate eggs in each one.

Leave the nests to chill in a refrigerator while the children help you to clear up and prepare for the next group's turn.

Support and extension

Younger children will need help to share the mixture and the eggs evenly between the cake cases. Ask older children for other ideas of ways that they can be considerate to others.

Further idea

■ Set up a system of group monitors, with each child having a specific daily task, such as putting lids on pens.

Celebration cake

What you need

Ingredients: 175g (6oz) self raising flour; 1½ tsp baking powder; 175g (6oz) caster sugar; 175g (6oz) soft margarine; 3 eggs; butter for greasing; 4 tbsp strawberry jam; 225g (8oz) icing sugar; 2–3 tbsp hot water.

Equipment: two sandwich tins; wooden spoons; large and small mixing bowls; sieve; palette knife; oven; cooling rack; icing pens in various colours; photocopiable sheet 'Cake decoration' on page 78; coloured pencils.

What to do

Choose a day when there is a reason to celebrate, such as a group occasion. Tell the children that you would like their help to make a special celebration cake.

Grease the sandwich tins, explaining to the children that this helps to stop the cakes from sticking to them, and weigh out the ingredients.

Sieve the flour and baking powder into a large mixing bowl. Add the sugar, margarine and eggs. Let the children take it in turns to mix the ingredients together with a wooden spoon. Then beat the mixture for three or four minutes until it is completely smooth.

Pour the mixture evenly between the two tins, levelling with a knife. Bake for around 20 minutes at 170°C (gas mark 3) until golden and firm to the touch.

Transfer the cakes to a wire cooling rack. When cool, spread jam on one of the cakes and sandwich them together. Mix up some icing sugar by combining the icing sugar and water and mixing to a smooth paste. Ask the children to help you to spread this evenly over the surface of the cake. Allow to set.

Now show the children the icing pens. Ask each child to decorate the cake with a pattern of their choice, using swirls, dots, zig-zags and so on.

Support and extension

For younger children, draw icing lines on the cake to divide it into quarters. Ask each child to keep their marks in their own quarter of the cake. Encourage older children to draft their pattern on a piece of paper first.

Further idea

■ Give each child a copy of photocopiable page 78 and ask them to complete the patterns on the cake template.

Raspberry sharbat

What you need

Ingredients: (makes four small cups) 50–75g (2–3 oz) raspberries plus 175g (6oz) puréed in a blender; 2 tsp lime juice; 2 cups water; fresh mint sprigs to garnish.

Equipment: large plastic lidded container suitable for freezing; freezer; spoons; four plastic glasses; colourful straws; serving spoon; bowls.

What to do

Ask the children to tell you about their favourite drinks. Are they allowed different drinks on special occasions? Encourage the children to take it in turns to speak and to listen to each other. Ask them to tell you about any special occasions that they have taken part in recently. What did they eat and drink?

Tell the children that they will be helping you to make and then taste a drink that is traditionally served in India on special occasions, and generally during the heat of the summer. It is called a *sharbat*, and they will be making a raspberry version.

Mix the raspberries, lime juice, sugar and water in a blender until relatively smooth. Place in a container and freeze.

When the drink is frozen remove it from the freezer and allow it to thaw a little. Ask the children to help you to use spoons to crush the sharbat to make a sort of slushy, snowy texture.

Place the puréed raspberries in the bottom of your four plastic glasses and pour the drink over the top. Garnish with mint sprigs, and add straws to make your very special drinks.

Suggest that the children pretend to hold a toy's tea or birthday party at which to serve their celebratory sharbat drinks!

Support and extension

Help younger children as they spoon out the mixture into the glasses. Talk with older children about the changes to the texture of the ingredients.

Further ideas

■ Find out about and make other Indian celebratory foods.

■ Look through food magazines for pictures of celebratory foods. Ask the children to draw a large table on a piece of paper and suggest that they cut out some tasty food pictures from the magazines to stick onto the table to make party pictures.

Charoset

What you need
Ingredients: 2 apples; 1 tsp cinnamon; 2 tbsp apple juice; 2 cups of raisins, chopped dates and chopped dried apricots.
Equipment: teaspoon; plates; bowls; mixing bowl; wooden spoon; grater.

What to do
Tell the children a little bit about the festival of Pesach. Explain that it is a time when Jewish people remember the bitterness of slavery and celebrate the joy of freedom. They do this in their homes with a special meal, and the food that they eat reminds them of the story.

Explain to the children that they are going to make a special dish called Charoset, which is traditionally eaten at the time of Pesach.

Make sure that each child has washed their hands carefully. Show them the ingredients for the Charoset and ask them to help you grate the apple into a bowl. Let them take a handful of each ingredient and arrange their ingredients in a pattern on a plate.

Once the children have had some time to experiment with pattern making, ask them to place all their ingredients into one large mixing bowl. Add the apple juice and cinnamon and mix together well. Spoon the mixture into individual bowls and enjoy it together.

Support and extension
Help younger children to make a face shape with their ingredients. For example, they may use the grated apple as hair and the apricots, raisins and dates as eyes and mouths. Encourage older children to describe the shapes and patterns they are making with their ingredients and why they have chosen them.

Further ideas
■ Read some stories about Passover, such as *Sam's Passover* by Lynne Hannigan (A&C Black).
■ Taste some of the other foods associated with the Passover meal such as matzos or unleavened bread.

LEARNING OBJECTIVES
STEPPING STONE
Show an interest in shape and space by playing with shapes or making arrangements with objects.

EARLY LEARNING GOAL
Talk about, recognise and recreate simple patterns. (MD)

GROUP SIZE
Four children at a time.

HOME LINKS
Invite any families that celebrate Pesach to come in and talk to the children about some of the other traditions relating to the festival.

Pinwheel sandwiches

What you need
Ingredients: slice of bread per child; cream cheese; thinly sliced ham; fruit chutney; butter.
Equipment: knives for spreading; cocktail sticks; spoons; serving plates; silver foil.

What to do
Choose a special occasion such as a festival or group event to make these appealing sandwiches.

Give each child a slice of bread with the crusts removed. Ask them to spread it carefully with butter and cream cheese. Add a slice or two of thin ham and a smear of chutney. Add some extra cream cheese to the long edges to help them to stick together. Now show the children how to roll the bread up in a long sausage shape. Wrap the rolls tightly in foil and chill for about 30 minutes.

Unwrap the rolls and ask the children to talk about the shape of the bread. Tell them that they are going to cut the roll into smaller rolls to make pinwheel sandwiches. How many smaller rolls do they think they will cut from their long roll? Help the children to slice their roll into smaller rounds. How many have they got now? Has everyone got the same number of sandwiches?

Provide older children with cocktail sticks and let them thread one or two pinwheels sideways onto the sticks. Lay them out on serving plates.

Support and extension
Use small slices of bread with younger children and limit the counting to five. Encourage older children to compare numbers with their friends.

Further ideas
■ Continue the counting work as you prepare more celebration food. For example, count out biscuits to put on a plate, the number of plates, cups and serviettes and so on.
■ Use different coloured fillings for making pinwheel sandwiches, such as jam, honey, marmite and cheese spread, chocolate spread and so on.

Cheese straws

What you need
Ingredients (makes 24 straws): sheet ready-rolled puff pastry; 100g (4oz) cheddar cheese, grated;1 tbsp tomato ketchup; 2 tsp milk.
Equipment: sharp knife (adult use); knife for spreading; grater; teaspoon; 2 lightly oiled baking trays; pastry brushes; jug or bowl; oven.

What to do
Make sure that the children have washed their hands and that your work surface is spotlessly clean. Show the children how you lightly oil or grease the baking trays. Ask the children why they think you are doing this.

Show the children the sheet of pastry. Trim off a little bit to give to each child and allow them some time to examine it. Can they see the different layers? What happens to it when they squeeze it or tear it?

Now cut the pastry sheet in half and spread one half with tomato ketchup and sprinkle the grated cheese on top. Press the other sheet firmly on top to make a sort of sandwich.

Cut the pastry sandwich into 12 strips. Give each child three strips and ask them to cut each strip in half. Show them how to gently twist the strips, then place them 3cm apart on the greased baking trays. Ask the children to brush their strips with a little milk. Bake in a pre-heated oven (around 200°C, gas mark 6) for about 10–12 minutes (until lightly browned).

Support and extension
Cut the strips for younger children and show how to twist them. Make, rather than buy, the puff pastry with older children. Encourage them to feel the texture of the pastry as it is being made.

Further ideas
■ Use another sheet of puff pastry to make some animal shapes. Spread the pastry with tomato ketchup and sprinkle with cheese, then use pastry cutters to cut out some animal shapes. Bake for around 10 minutes.
■ Make some other pastry based party snacks such as vol-au-vents and sausage rolls.

Fruit punch

What you need
Ingredients: 2 oranges; 2 lemons; 1 large bottle sparkling mineral water; 300ml (½ pint) apple juice; 2 tbsp undiluted blackcurrant drink; handful of strawberries.
Equipment: two large jugs; cups; a sharp knife (adult use); colander; large tablespoon or similar for mixing; two shallow plastic, lidded containers suitable for freezing; freezer.

What to do
Explain to the children that they are going to help you to make a delicious fizzy party drink. Ask them what their favourite party drinks are. Tell them that this drink will be fruity and will have some very special fruit ice-cubes to keep it cool.

Show the children the ingredients and ask them to help you to wash all the fruits. Slice one orange and one lemon. Ask the children to lay out the orange and lemon slices in the bottom of two shallow plastic containers, so that they are not overlapping. Explain that you are going to put these containers, with their lids on, into the freezer to make some fruit ice.

Around the time that the fruit has frozen (around three to four hours depending on your freezer) chop up the remaining orange and lemon into slices and slice the strawberries.

Pour the liquids into one or two large jugs and give them a mix. Add the sliced fruits. Just before serving the drink remove the frozen fruit slices from the freezer. Give the children the opportunity to examine the fruits and talk about how they have changed. Add the fruit ice to the jugs to cool the fruit punch.

Let the children help to pour and share out the tasty fruit-iced drink.

Support and extension
Younger children will need some help to pour from a heavy jug. Let older children suggest some other ingredients to add to the punch.

Further ideas
■ Make frozen fruit juice ice-lollies by pouring the children's favourite juices into lolly moulds and then freezing.
■ Make fruity ice cubes by placing pieces of fruit such as raspberries in the squares in an ice-cube tray and then pouring over water or fruit juice to freeze.

Marzipan fruits

What you need
Ingredients: pack of ready made marzipan (size dependent on how many fruits you wish to make); yellow, red, green and orange food colouring; a little water in a cup.

Equipment: clear plastic film; fine, clean paint brushes; kitchen scissors; knives; kitchen towel; plate for each child; small boxes; red or green crepe paper; glue sticks; scissors; sticky tape.

What to do
Check that none of the children have a nut allergy before handling (or eating) the marzipan. Prepare some of the little marzipan fruits to show the children (see below). Explain that they are sometimes made and given as gifts at Christmas time. Tell the children that they will each make their own basket of fruits to take home with them.

Give each child a small box and let them choose some red or green paper. Help them to cover their boxes, fixing the paper with glue or sticky tape. Place a small piece of kitchen towel inside each box to line it and put to one side.

Now show the children the ingredients – the ready made marzipan and the range of food colours. Knead the marzipan, with the children's help, to make it soft.

Start by making some bananas. Give each child a small piece of marzipan and show them how to roll it into a ball and then mould the ball into a thin banana shape. Curve it slightly and flatten it along one side, making a tiny stalk shape at one end.

Give each child a plate covered in cling film and ask them to put their bananas onto their plates. Now make some apples and oranges from the marzipan, flattening the tops of the ball shapes slightly and adding features such as stalks.

When the children have made a selection of fruits let them take it in turns to use the fine brush with one of the colours. Paint all the fruits of one colour first, then clean the brush ready for the next colour.

Leave the marzipan fruits to dry, then transfer them from the plates to the baskets ready to take home.

Support and extension
Younger children will find it easier to make slightly bigger fruits. Challenge older children to make at least four different kinds of fruits and perhaps add some textural details.

Further idea
■ Make marzipan Christmas trees by using a Christmas tree pastry cutter to cut out shapes. Paint the trees with green food colouring and then press little silver confectionery balls into the branches as baubles.

LEARNING OBJECTIVES
STEPPING STONE
Manipulate materials to achieve a planned effect.

EARLY LEARNING GOAL
Handle tools, objects, construction and malleable materials safely and with increasing control. (PD)

GROUP SIZE
Small groups at a time.

HOME LINKS
Take home the little baskets of fruit as Christmas presents for parents and carers.

Tasty hedgehogs!

What you need
Ingredients (makes two hedgehogs): 1 large grapefruit; pineapple chunks; cherry tomatoes; chunks of cooked sausage; cubes of cheese; chunks of cucumber; 2 olives per hedgehog (as eyes).
Equipment: cocktail sticks; serving plates; sharp knife (adult use).

What to do
These colourful hedgehog treats make great centrepieces for an end of term party or other celebration.

Work with two or three children at a time. Cut a large grapefruit in half and turn it upside down on a serving plate. Explain to the children that they are going to make a colourful prickly hedgehog with some tasty colourful goodies to eat on each spine (cocktail stick)!

Show the children the selection of foods that they can add to the hedgehog's spines. Talk about the range of colours, shapes and textures of the foods. Explain that they should use two olives as his eyes, but that they can choose any colours and combinations for the rest of the hedgehog's features.

Allow the children to cover the hedgehog with their own choice of a colourful assortment of goodies. Encourage them to make aesthetic judgements, for example, making sure that there are not too many gaps and that there is an even spread of colours.

Support and extension
Supervise younger children as they work, making sure that they handle the cocktail sticks carefully and appropriately! Suggest that older children create a specific pattern, using rings of colour, or repeating sequences, for example.

Further ideas
■ Read the story *The Hedgehog's Balloon* by Nick Butterworth (Harper Collins). In the story, Percy the Park Keeper fixes corks onto the hedgehog's spikes to stop him from bursting his balloon!
■ Make bunting for the party by giving each child a triangular flag shape to decorate in bright colours. Attach all the flags with sticky tape to a length of string ready to hang up.

Sweet treats

In this final chapter you will find recipes with great child-appeal – all based around sweet ingredients. Although the recipes are sweet in taste, many use fruit and other fresh ingredients and provide healthy and imaginative ways of satisfying any sweet cravings!

Bread and butter pudding

What you need

Ingredients: 2 slices white bread (crusts removed); butter for spreading and greasing; 300ml milk; 1 tbsp single cream; 2 eggs; 1 tbsp caster sugar; ¼ teaspoon vanilla essence; pinch ground nutmeg; boiling water.

Equipment: knives; four heatproof dishes (125ml capacity); 2 baking dishes (big enough to fit two of the heatproof dishes inside); kettle; jug; whisk; oven; spoons.

What to do

Set out the ingredients on the table (except the boiling water) and ask the children to identify each item. What do they think they could make with these ingredients? Show them the small heatproof bowls and tell them that they will be cooking the ingredients inside these bowls to make puddings. Grease the bowls and explain how this will stop the puddings from sticking to the sides.

Ask the children if they have ever tasted bread and butter pudding and briefly explain how it is made. What do the children think will happen to the bread when it has liquid poured onto it?

Now let the children help to prepare the dishes. Ask them to butter the two slices of bread. Cut each slice into four triangles and divide them amongst the four dishes. Let the children take turns to whisk together the milk, cream, eggs, sugar and vanilla in a jug. Pour the mixture over the bread in each dish and then sprinkle on a little nutmeg.

Ask the children to watch as you place the dishes into a baking dish and pour enough boiling water to come half way up the sides of the dishes. Bake in a pre-heated moderate oven for about 20 minutes (until they set).

Look at the finished puddings together and comment on how the liquid has set. Taste the puddings when they have cooled and ask the children to describe the texture and taste of the bread.

Support and extension

Let younger children feel the difference between two pieces of bread – one soaked in milk and the other dry. Ask older children to remember and talk about the process of making the pudding.

Further idea

■ Try out and discuss some other ways of cooking bread with the children.

Strawberry frozen yogurt

LEARNING OBJECTIVES
STEPPING STONE
Take initiatives and manage developmentally appropriate tasks.

EARLY LEARNING GOAL
Select and use activities and resources independently.
(PSED)

GROUP SIZE
Up to four children.

What you need
Ingredients: 2×150g cartons strawberry yogurt; 125g (4oz) fresh strawberries.
Equipment: freezer; food processor; selection of containers including a large plastic container; forks; children's knives; mixing bowl; mixing spoon; serving bowls; suitable and unsuitable containers for the yogurt.

What to do
Ask the children if they have ever tasted frozen yogurt. If so, can they describe it? If not, what do they think it will taste like? Explain that they are going to make some of their own frozen strawberry yogurt now. How do they think it could be made? Show them the ingredients. How will the yogurt be frozen?

Once the children have decided that they will mix and then put the ingredients in a freezer, ask them to consider what they will put the mixture in. Show them your range of containers (including some clearly unsuitable containers, such as paper bags, saucepans and carrier bags). Help them to choose one large or two or three small plastic containers with lids.

Now start to make the frozen yogurt together. Let the children use children's knives to carefully chop the strawberries, then help them to place the strawberries into the food processor to purée. Pour the puréed strawberries into a bowl and mix together with the yogurt.

Pour the mixture into the chosen container(s) and place them in the freezer. When the mixture is frozen around the sides (time dependent on the efficiency of your freezer), break up the ice crystals with a fork and mix once more. Return to the freezer until fully frozen.

Talk about the finished product together as you enjoy it! Does it taste how the children imagined it would?

Support and extension
Chop the strawberries in advance for younger children. Encourage older children to work as independently as possible. Ask them to predict changes in the strawberries, such as texture, temperature, colour and taste.

Further ideas
■ Have a frozen yogurt and ice cream tasting session. Find out the group's favourite taste and flavour.
■ Make some frozen yogurt lollies by following the recipe and then freezing the mixture in ice-lolly moulds.

HOME LINKS
Suggest that the children try out a different flavoured version at home (they could use apricot yogurt and puréed apricots, for example).

Fruit jelly

What you need

Ingredients: packet of fruit-flavoured jelly; medium tin of fruit cocktail in fruit juice (without pineapple, as it prevents jelly from setting); water.

Equipment: kettle; measuring jug; spoons; serving bowl; small bowls; fridge.

What to do

Tell the children that you are going to describe some foods to them and that you would like them to try and guess what food you are talking about. Start with some easy descriptions, such as 'It's a fruit, it's yellow and curvy. Monkeys like to eat it!' Try to use as many descriptive words as you can. Finish the game by describing jelly, for example, saying that it is a '… wibbly, wobbly fruit-flavoured pudding that often falls off your spoon!'.

Tell the children that they will be helping you to make a fruit jelly. Do the children think the jelly will be smooth when the fruit has been added?

Follow the instructions on the packet of jelly, substituting some of the water for the fruit juice drained from the can of fruit. Add the fruit pieces to the bowl of jelly as it cools. Refrigerate until set.

Let the children taste the jelly. Ask them to describe the texture and appearance of the jelly. Is it as slippery as normal jelly?

Support and extension

Show younger children some examples of food as you describe them. Let them take turns to hold the foods and encourage them to describe the way that they feel. Invite older children to describe foods from their memories for each other to guess.

Further ideas

■ Hold a food tasting session, encouraging the children to use words such as 'spicy, sweet, runny, sticky' and so on to describe the foods they are tasting.
■ Make a list of wobbly foods such as trifle, blancmange, jelly, crème caramel, soft meringue and so on.

Fruity dip

LEARNING OBJECTIVES
STEPPING STONE
Begin to use talk instead of action to rehearse, reorder and reflect on past experience, linking significant events from own experience and from stories, paying attention to sequence and how events lead into one another.

EARLY LEARNING GOAL
Use talk to organise, sequence and clarify thinking, ideas, feelings and events. (CLL)

GROUP SIZE
The whole group for the discussion; small groups for the cookery activity.

What you need
Ingredients: 250g cream cheese and equal quantities of fromage frais, Greek yogurt and fruit purée (you can make your own apricot purée, for example, by stewing dried apricots in water and then puréeing them in a food processor); chunks of fresh fruit for dipping, such as apple, banana, mango and strawberries.

Equipment: large mixing bowl; spoons; knives for chopping fruit (adult use); serving dishes; large plates; clear plastic film; posters and pictures of healthy food; plastic fruits and vegetables; examples of packaging of healthy foods; display table; photocopiable sheet 'Five a day' on page 68.

What to do
Arrange to have a healthy eating focus for a week. Set up a display table with the pictures and posters, healthy food packaging, plastic fruits and vegetables and so on.

Talk to the children about healthy living and find out their thoughts on what foods are healthy or unhealthy. Sing the 'Five a day' song from photocopiable page 68 together.

Explain that they are going to help you to make a healthy yogurt-based dip that is good for dipping fresh fruits into. Tell them that they will be inviting their parents or carers to come in and try the results!

Make the dip with small groups of children by mixing all the ingredients together in a large mixing bowl. Spoon the dip into some serving bowls, then arrange the chunks of fruit on plates with the dip in the centre. Refrigerate, covered with clear plastic film until required.

Invite parents and carers to come in and sample the dips and fruits at the end of the session. Suggest that the children explain the process of making the dip to their parents.

Support and extension
Help younger children to remember and explain how the dip was made. Encourage older children to tell the whole process of making the dip, from measuring out ingredients to putting it in the fridge.

HOME LINKS
Ask the children to bring in from home any food packaging from popular brands of healthy eating products.

Further idea
■ Make a savoury dip to taste at the same time, such as the 'French onion dip' on page 30.

Peachy egg custard

What you need

Ingredients: 70g (2½oz) plain flour; 70g (2½oz) sugar; 6–8 tinned peach (or pear or apricot) halves, drained; 3 eggs; 250ml (8 floz) full-fat milk; 1 tsp vanilla essence; butter for greasing; icing sugar for sprinkling.
Equipment: selection of plastic shapes (include some that will and some that won't tessellate); rectangular sheets of paper; oven; 1-litre capacity ovenproof dish; blender; serving bowls and spoons.

What to do

Give the children your selection of plastic shapes and ask them to play freely with them, making patterns and fitting them together. Next give them a rectangular sheet of paper and invite them to arrange the shapes in different ways on the sheet. Can they find the best shapes to use to cover the paper completely with no gaps?

Explain that you would now like their help to cover the bottom of your greased dish with fruit pieces. Ask them to look at the shape of the fruit pieces. Do they think they will be able to cover the bottom of the dish without leaving any gaps? Let them try and see (ask them to place the fruit cut-side up). Talk about the results together.

Now combine the eggs, flour, milk and sugar in a blender. Pour the mixture over the fruits and then place the dish in a preheated oven at 180°C (gas mark 4) for around 40 minutes (until the custard is set and golden in colour).

Sprinkle the finished dish with icing sugar before enjoying.

Support and extension

Show younger children how squares can be put next to each other without any gaps, but how circles, when placed together, leave small gaps showing. Ask older children to draw around their tessellating shape pictures.

LEARNING OBJECTIVES
STEPPING STONE
Show an interest in shape and space by playing with shapes or making arrangements with objects.

EARLY LEARNING GOAL
Use developing mathematical ideas and methods to solve practical problems. (MD)

GROUP SIZE
Two children at a time.

Further ideas

■ Make some printed tessellating shape pictures by pressing shapes into sponges soaked in paint and then printing arrangements of shapes on a separate sheet of paper.
■ Look at examples of fabrics, wallpapers and other printed material that show different arrangements of shapes, some that tessellate and some that don't.

HOME LINKS
Ask the children to look around their homes to find examples of shape patterns.

Fruity kebabs

What you need
Ingredients: chunks of fresh fruit such as strawberries, apples, bananas, pineapple, apricots, plums and so on.
Equipment: knife for chopping fruit (adult use); bowls; kebab skewers (bamboo would be best for young children); photocopiable sheet 'How many fruits' on page 79; coloured pencils.

What to do
Provide each child with the photocopiable sheet and pencils. Talk about what the pictures show. Explain that when you pierce fruits (or other items of food) onto skewers they are called kebabs.

Ask the children to identify the fruits in the pictures and then to count the number of fruit pieces on each kebab. Let them count each one and write the number underneath, colouring them in if they wish. Talk about which kebabs have the most, same and least pieces of fruit and which kebab has the most grapes and so on.

Now tell the children that they are going to make their own real fruity kebabs. Let them select their own fruits and help them to slide them gently onto the skewers. Ask the children to count the fruits on their kebabs and compare them with each other. Which fruit was the most popular? Who has the most fruits on their kebab?

Finally, eat and enjoy the kebabs.

Support and extension
Limit the numbers to six or seven pieces for younger children and help them to count accurately by pointing to each fruit as they say a number. Suggest that older children re-count the number of fruits on their kebabs after a couple of minutes to find out who has eaten the most pieces of fruit so far!

Further ideas
■ Provide beads and threading laces and continue the counting and comparing work as the children make necklaces.
■ Set challenges for the children, such as asking them to make a kebab with seven pieces, using three different fruits; or to make four different kebabs using six pieces of fruit.

Chocolate slices

What you need

Ingredients: 60g (2½oz) plain chocolate; 50g (2oz) unsalted butter; 1 tbsp double cream; 1 tbsp golden syrup; 100g (4oz) digestive biscuits; 25g (1oz) raisins; 30–40g (1½oz) chopped glacé cherries.

Equipment: heatproof (glass or ceramic) mixing bowl; saucepan of water; hob; wooden spoon; spoons; potato masher or slotted spoon; large mixing bowl; 10cm² tin; aluminium foil; fridge.

What to do

Choose a week when you are particularly pleased with the children's behaviour and explain that you are going to help them to make a delicious treat. Stress that they are going to need to be expert cooks to make this recipe, as it uses a range of different techniques. Ask the children if they can think of any techniques used in cookery and food preparation (such as mashing, mixing and stirring).

Ask the children to help break up the chocolate roughly into squares. Place the pieces in a heatproof bowl, along with the cream, butter and syrup. Tell the children that you will melt the ingredients by steaming them above a pan of simmering water. Gently stir the mixture until it is melted. Talk about the techniques you have all used so far.

Meanwhile ask the children to roughly break up the biscuits and put them all in a large mixing bowl along with the raisins and chopped cherries. Pour the melted mixture on top and ask the children to mix it all together.

Line your square tin with foil and then spoon the mixture into the tin. Ask the children to take it in turns to press the mixture down firmly with a potato masher or the back of a slotted spoon. Place in the fridge to set (around one hour). Cut into slices and serve to the children.

Support and extension

Younger children may need some help as they pour the mixture. Ask older children to think of all the techniques that you used to make the chocolate slices (such as melting, mixing, pressing, pouring and cutting).

Further idea

■ Fill your home corner with a range of safe cooking utensils and equipment that will encourage the children to role-play some different cooking techniques (such as mashing, stirring and whisking).

LEARNING OBJECTIVES
STEPPING STONE
Use simple tools and techniques competently and appropriately.

EARLY LEARNING GOAL
Select the tools and techniques they need to shape, assemble and join materials they are using. (KUW)

GROUP SIZE
Four children.

HOME LINKS
Ask the children to tell you what foods they are given as special treats at home.

Baked apples

What you need

Ingredients: 4 cooking apples; 50g (2oz) mixed dried fruit or sultanas; 200ml apple juice; knob of butter for each apple; 2–3 tsp brown sugar.
Equipment: apple corer and sharp knife (adult use only); ovenproof dish; jug; spoons; oven; photocopiable page 80.

What to do

Ask the children if they have ever heard the traditional saying 'An apple a day keeps the doctor away'. What do they think it means? Talk a bit more about eating healthily.

Tell the children that they will each make their own special baked apple with you. Show them the cooking apples and ask them if they know which bits of the apple are not good to eat (the core and the pips). Show them how you can take out the core (and pips) with the corer. Score each apple a couple of times with a knife to stop the skin bursting when it is cooked.

Ask the children to stuff their own apples with some dried fruit or sultanas before placing the apples in an ovenproof dish. Pour the apple juice around the apples and then ask the children to sprinkle their own apples with some brown sugar. Dot the apples with a little butter before placing them in a pre-heated oven at 180–190°C, gas mark 4–5. Bake for around 35–40 minutes (depending on the size of your apples) until the flesh is soft.

Wait for the apples to cool down before tasting them (as dried fruit retains heat for a long time).

Finish by practising the rhyme on photocopiable page 80 together.

Support and extension

Young children will enjoy stuffing their apples with fruits. Make sure they taste samples of the mixed fruits before they use them, in case they prefer to use just sultanas or raisins. Challenge older children to learn the rhyme in the time taken to cook the apples!

Further idea

■ Find out what the children's favourite fruits are. Put the results into a bar chart for the children to interpret.

LEARNING OBJECTIVES

STEPPING STONE

Show awareness of a range of healthy practices with regard to eating, sleeping and hygiene.

EARLY LEARNING GOAL

Recognise the importance of keeping healthy and those things which contribute to this. (PD)

GROUP SIZE

Four children.

HOME LINKS

Give each child a copy of the photocopiable rhyme to take home and enjoy with their parents or carers.

Creative desserts

What you need

Ingredients: tinned peach or pear half per child; packet of instant dessert whip and fresh milk as per instructions; fresh fruit pieces such as mandarin segments; grapes; chunks of apple, pineapple or banana.

Equipment: jug; mixing bowl; fork or whisk; spoons; knife for chopping fruit (adult use); large plate.

What to do

Ask the children if they have ever tasted an instant dessert whip (or similar). Do they know how it is made? Explain that you would like their help to make some. Make it together, following the instructions on the packet.

Tell the children that they are going to use the instant dessert whip to make some funny faces to eat! Give each child a pear or peach half and ask them to spoon some set instant dessert whip onto the cut side so that it fills the hole. Show the children your cut up fruits (if preparing in advance, sprinkle with some lemon juice to stop the fruit from discolouring). Demonstrate how to make a funny face by adding a mandarin segment mouth, grape eyes and so on. Now invite the children to have a turn.

Talk about all the funny faces together. Which faces look happy, sad, scary and so on? Provide the children with spoons and let them enjoy eating their creations!

Support and extension

Younger children may need reminding to include a nose and ears, or hair for example, as many will just add eyes. Challenge older children to make specific kinds of face, such as happy, scary or sad.

Further ideas

■ Make some other instant dessert whip creations using different flavours, fruit pieces, sweets and slices of cake such as swiss roll. Challenge the children to make animal or monster faces!

■ Make some savoury pizza faces in a similar way, this time using pieces of ham, cheese, tomatoes and sweetcorn.

LEARNING OBJECTIVES
STEPPING STONE
Work creatively on a large or small scale.

EARLY LEARNING GOAL
Explore colour, texture, shape, form and space in two or three dimensions. (CD)

GROUP SIZE
Up to five children at a time.

HOME LINKS
Invite parents to contribute any ideas they have for making fun healthy food. Suggest that they come in and make them with the children.

Ice cream and fruit sundaes

What you need

Ingredients: 1 sachet dessert topping mix and milk as per instructions; 4 cartons ready made jelly; vanilla ice cream; 2 tins (300g) summer fruits drained in a sieve over a bowl; 4 pairs fresh cherries; 4 tbsp maple syrup or other ice cream dessert topping.

Equipment: 4 ice cream sundae dishes (8floz); sieve; measuring jug; whisk; ice cream scoop; tablespoons; spoons. For the role-play area: serving counter, menus, price-lists; pretend ice cream and scoops; table with tablecloth and chairs, serviettes, spoons and so on.

What to do

With the children's help, set up your role-play area as an ice cream parlour (see suggestions in equipment, above). Next to the children's ice cream parlour set out the ingredients and equipment needed to make real ice cream sundaes.

Explain to the children that they will each make their own ice cream sundae that they can eat in the role-play area.

Give each child a sundae dish and suggest to them how to make their sundaes, for example, they may include some ice cream, jelly, fruit, topping and sauce, as well as decorating it with a pair of cherries.

Let the children experiment with the ingredients, adding the components of their sundae in an order that appeals to them! Draw their attention to the way the ingredients mix together and how they look. Ask them to describe their creations as they work. Encourage them to appreciate that the topping, sauce and cherries will make attractive finishing touches.

Once their sundaes are finished let them take them into the role-play area to enjoy. Choose another child to act as the shop owner, providing the 'customers' with serviettes, spoons and so on.

Support and extension

Younger children will enjoy the experience of mixing, pouring and creating and will probably have less regard for the aesthetic appeal of their sundae – this is fine! Encourage older children to plan their sundaes before they begin.

Further idea

■ Take digital pictures of the children's creations and use them to print exciting menus and posters for your ice cream parlour!

Parcel fillings

Try these tasty fillings.

Tuna crunch

Mashed tuna with chopped cucumber and mayonnaise.

Sweet cheese

Cottage cheese, grated cheddar or cream cheese mixed
with chopped pineapple or peach pieces.

Egg mayo

Chopped hard-boiled egg with mayonnaise and cress.

Hamslaw

Coleslaw mixed with chopped ham and grated cheese.

Banana mad

Chopped or mashed banana with honey.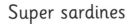

Super sardines

Mashed sardines mixed with a little tomato sauce.

Cheese and tomato

Grated cheese with sliced tomatoes.

Chicken and apple

Chopped cooked chicken with grated apple.

Five a day

(Tune: 'Here We Go Round the Mulberry Bush'.)
Adapt the names and foods as appropriate to your children.

We must eat fruit and vegetables, vegetables, vegetables,
We must eat fruit and vegetables
Every single day

Peter likes to eat red peppers, eat red peppers, eat red peppers,
Peter likes to eat red peppers
Let's try some today

Naveed likes to eat sweetcorn, eat sweetcorn, eat sweetcorn
Naveed likes to eat sweetcorn
Let's eat some today

Katie likes to eat tomatoes, eat tomatoes, eat tomatoes
Katie likes to eat tomatoes
Let's cook some today

William likes to eat mange tout, eat mange tout, eat mange tout
William likes to eat mange tout
Let's chop some today

Manjit likes to eat broccoli, eat broccoli, eat broccoli
Manjit likes to eat broccoli
Every single day

Sally Scott

Fruit match

Draw lines to match the dried and fresh fruits.

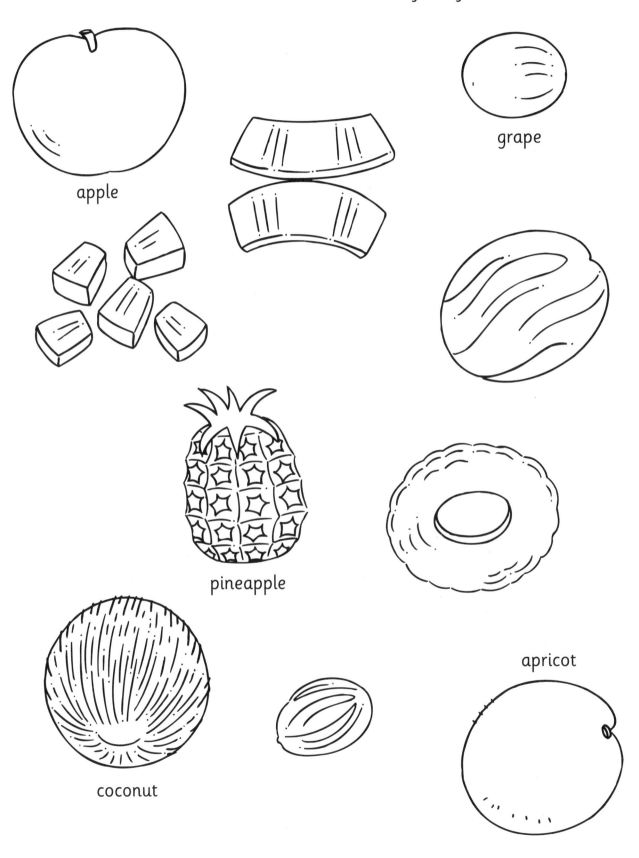

apple

grape

pineapple

coconut

apricot

Traffic light fruits

Food shapes

Talk about the shapes of all these foods.

Welsh rarebit

Ingredients
125g (4oz) mature cheddar cheese (grated)
125g (4oz) cream cheese
1 tablespoon butter
1 teaspoon Worcestershire sauce
1 teaspoon chopped fresh chives
pinch of mild chilli powder
thick slices bread

Method
■ Beat the cream cheese and butter together in a large mixing bowl until blended.
■ Lightly toast the bread on both sides.
■ Add the grated cheese, Worcestershire sauce, chopped chives and chilli to the cream cheese and butter mixture. Combine well.
■ Spread the mixture onto the bread and toast until lightly browned and bubbling.

Pizza topping challenge

Give each pizza a topping. Try to make each pizza look different.
You may use:

mushroom   cheese

ham   tomato

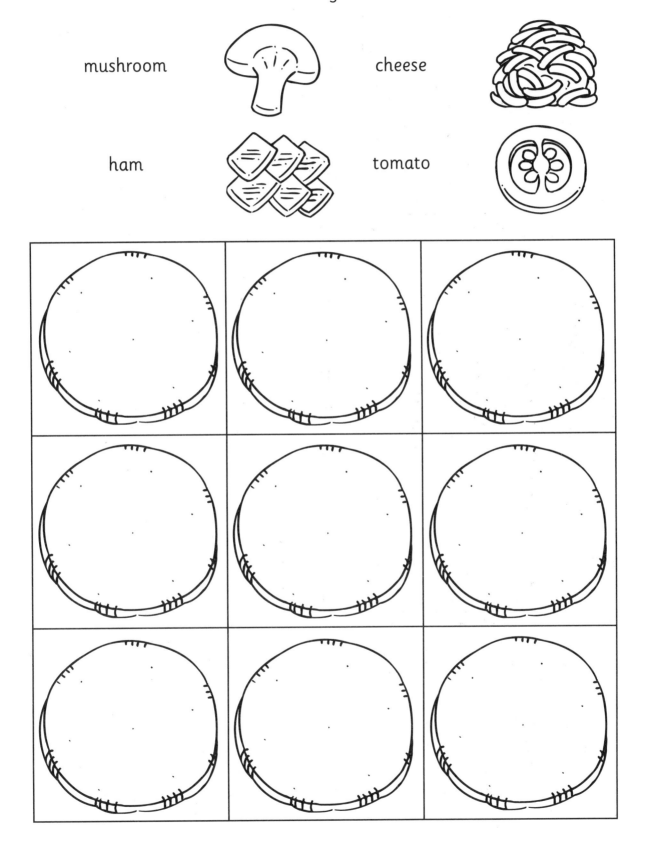

Technology cards

Cut out and talk about the pictures.

My dip recipe

Ingredients

What to do

SCHOLASTIC

What begins with b?

Colour those things that begin with 'b'.

Muffin mix up

Cut out the pictures and put them in the right order.

Cake decoration

Trace over the patterns on the cake.

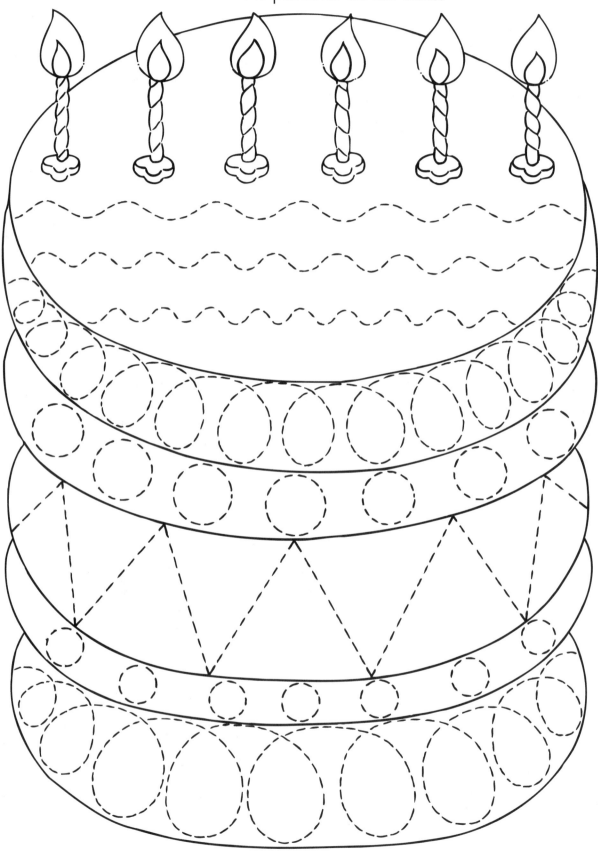

How many fruits?

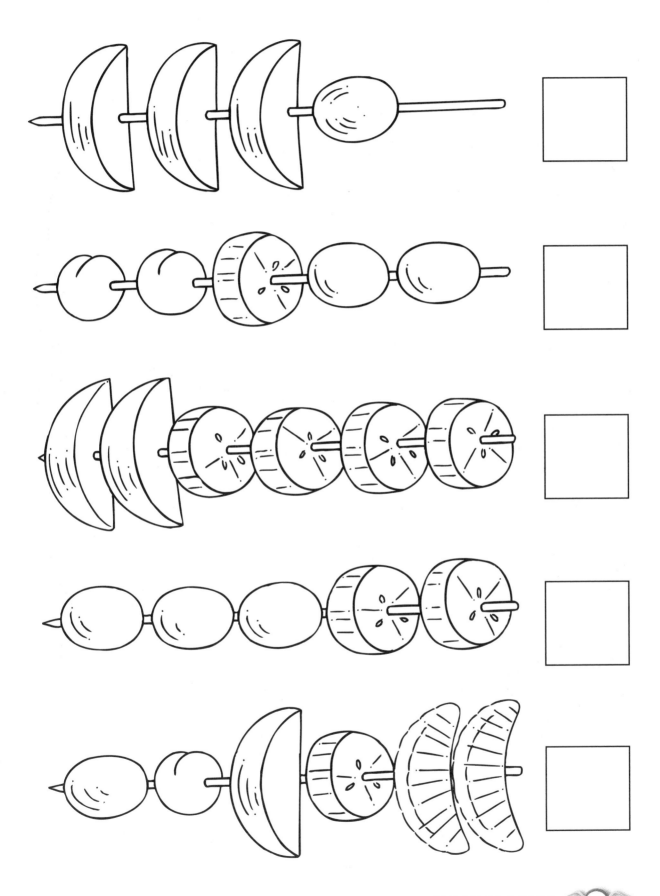

SCHOLASTIC **79**

Apples are...

Apples are red.
Apples are green.
Apples are shiny.
Apples can gleam.

Apples are juicy.
Apples are sweet.
Apples are healthy
And good to eat!

Brenda Williams